DEESIDE

DEESIDE

BY

ALEX. INKSON McCONNOCHIE

With a new Introduction
by
D. J. Withrington M.A. M.Ed.

Republished EP Publishing Ltd., 1972
from the 3rd edition published Aberdeen, 1900

East Ardsley, Wakefield,
Yorkshire, England

ISBN 0 85409 772 4

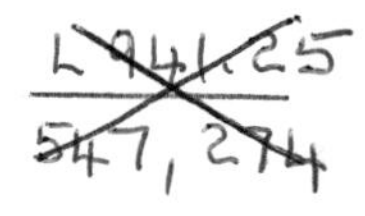

Please address all enquiries to EP Publishing Ltd.
(address as above)

Reprinted in Great Britain by
Scolar Press Limited, Menston, Yorkshire

INTRODUCTION

by D. J. WITHRINGTON M.A. M.ED.
Director, University of Aberdeen Centre for Scottish Studies

For all his publications and despite the fact that he must have been well-known in Aberdeen and its neighbourhood at the turn of this century, Alexander Inkson McConnochie is a rather shadowy figure. When he died in London in 1936, he had already been away from North-East Scotland for a quarter of a century and, at the age of 86 years, had outlived a great many of his Aberdeen friends and contemporaries. Thus, the obituaries of him in the local press and periodicals tend to be meagre in those personal details which are so valuable to historians; and, unfortunately, McConnochie seems to have drawn little or no published comment on himself in the period when he was prominent in the locality.

We know that he was born on Speyside, at Rothes in Morayshire, and was schooled at Inchberry near Fochabers and at Oyne in Aberdeenshire, before taking up an apprenticeship in an Aberdeen law office. It was in Aberdeen that he set up in business as an accountant and law agent, becoming in 1877 an associate member of the Society of Accountants in England (after 1880 the Institute of Chartered Accountants of England and Wales); he seems, for whatever reason, never to have been a member of the Institute of Chartered Accountants of Scotland. McConnochie is credited with only one legal publication, *Marriage and Registration, founded on Bisset-Smith's 'Vital Registration'*, in 1909. But freemasonry drew him oftener into print, for he helped to edit the *Aberdeen Masonic Reporter* after 1879 and shared the writing of a volume on *Craft Masonry* in 1901. His main publishing interests, however, lay elsewhere: in the exploration of the North-East and Central Highlands of Scotland.

In 1885 Lewis Smith of Aberdeen published McConnochie's *Ben Muich Dhui and his Neighbours: a Guide to the Cairngorm Mountains* which was dedicated to seventeen of his 'Cairngorm friends and companions . . . in remembrance of many pleasant excursions between Braemar and the Spey'. In it the author recounts his early blunderings across the Cairngorms because he had had no suitable guidebook: *Ben Muich Dhui* was his attempt to provide others with the kind of help he had failed to find. McConnochie was alive to the importance of sharing experiences in hill-walking and mountaineering; and when, on 23 June 1887, he and five companions climbed Ben Muich Dhui to let off fireworks in celebration of Queen Victoria's jubilee, they discussed the possibilities of forming a Cairngorm Club. The Club was formally incorporated on 9 January 1889, with McConnochie as secretary; and when it was decided to publish a journal in July 1893 he became its editor and retained both posts until he left Aberdeen for Glasgow in 1910.

Ben Muich Dhui was plainly intended for his hill-walking friends, and so were two other shilling guides which followed soon after—*Bennachie* (1890) and *Lochnagar* (1891)—and also 'two interesting little pamphlets prepared . . . in anticipation of excursions of the Cairngorm Club' to *Ben a Bhuird and Ben Avon* and *Ben Rinne* in 1891. McConnochie's distaste for the increasingly 'professional' mountaineering of the early 1890s is to be seen in *Lochnagar*. A reviewer in the *Scottish Mountaineering Club Journal* (vol. ii, January 1892) commented: 'Mr. McConnochie is a lover of nature and a hillman of the best type, and most of us will agree with his dictum when he says

"I hold that the true mountaineer is not the man who boasts of the number of peaks he has placed to his credit: the ideal hillman is one who thoroughly enjoys a day *on* the mountains, not hurrying and toiling up a Ben with the single purpose of rushing down again".' McConnochie's guides were, accordingly, much more than a climber's handbook to mountain routes and were 'full of information—traditional, legendary and scientific—that is likely to be of interest'.

Two Aberdeen publishers, Wyllie and Lewis Smith, seem to have vied with each other to persuade McConnochie to write more general guides to the district, not so much for the resident hiker as for the increasing numbers of tourists who came to Aberdeen en route for the west and north. Thus, in 1893 came, at a shilling again, the first edition of *Deeside* from Wyllie. It was quickly republished in an expanded version by Lewis Smith in 1895 and incorporated an early Smith guide to the area. In 1900 a third and better edition was issued and it is this which is reprinted here.

It hardly needs to be said that the book was a success. And once its author had begun writing for a more general market he was indefatigable. The tourists' appetite for books on Deeside was fed again and again—*Queen Victoria's Highland Home and its Vicinity* (1897) was followed by *The Royal Dee* (1898) and then *Views of Royal Deeside* (1903). And in the ten years after 1900 there were other guides and picture-books galore—on Donside, Ellon and district, Strathspey, Buchan, Inverness, Aberdeen itself, Aviemore and district, Kincardineshire and Speyside.

Yet, a little surprisingly perhaps, all this activity ceased once McConnochie left Aberdeen: possibly a sign that he had been driven along by the local publishers rather than an indication that he was running out of subject-matter. When he published again, and this was not until the 1920s and after he had moved to London, it reflected a related but different interest. In 1923 there appeared what became a very well-known and highly regarded study of *The Deer and Deer Forests of Scotland*, followed in 1924 by *Deerstalking in Scotland.* His last book, *Deer Forest Life*, was published in 1932, and it was said that he was working on a volume on birds in the Scottish deer forests when he died. The seriousness of these studies is perhaps best seen in the fact that he was elected, during the period he lived in London, to a Fellowship of the Zoological Society.

Deeside, particularly in its second and third editions, was well received by local reviewers. Because it was intended for incoming tourists with no information at all about the region, or so it would seem, McConnochie removed from it that emphasis on geology and botany which marked the earlier upper Deeside guides: this largely gave way to expansive descriptions, to the inclusion of much local history and legend and also of poetry with good local reference. In this latter feature *Deeside* gained greatly from its having encompassed James Brown's *The Guide to the Highlands of Deeside*, which was first published by Lewis Smith in 1831 and was reissued with notes and other additions many times thereafter. As the 1869 edition of the *Guide* explained, Brown was only the 'reputed' author: it had really been compiled 'in a frolicsome mood during a holiday at Ballater' by Dr. Joseph Robertson, soon to be an antiquary of note throughout Scotland, a remarkable historical scholar who was already the author of a very good local history in *The Book of Bon Accord* (1839). The combination of McConnochie and Robertson provided, and still provides, a fine introduction to Deeside.

The guide shows its age now, of course. There is, for example, no longer a Deeside railway to Ballater although it was described in 1900 as 'one of the most profitable and beneficial enterprises in the North'; if the expected population expansion south of the river from Aberdeen did not take place in the nineteenth century it has done so since; Broad Street in Aberdeen, complained of in 1900 as being quite incorrectly named, has succumbed to the bulldozers and now more nearly meets the assumptions which a visitor might make about it; the Queen Anne wing of Crathes Castle, thanks to a recent fire, has returned to its original two storeys and no longer has the three mentioned by McConnochie; and so on.

But there is little or no loss here; or, at least, whatever loss there might be is nicely outweighed by the added interest and the historical value of the now dated comments about transportation or agriculture or buildings. McConnochie's *Deeside* is itself now a historical source, but the passage of seventy years has not notably reduced its value to the present-day tourist who demands a 'here-and-now' guide. When his *Lochnagar* was reviewed in 1892, it was said that 'those who don't know the area cannot do better than place themselves under Mr. McConnochie's guidance'. That might well have been repeated for *Deeside* in 1900, and there is a very good case for similarly welcoming its reprint in 1972.

JUNE 1972

DEESIDE

DEESIDE

BY

ALEX. INKSON McCONNOCHIE

THIRD EDITION

(With which is incorporated "The Deeside Guide")

ABERDEEN

LEWIS SMITH & SON

1900

CONTENTS

(For List of Illustrations and Ballads see next page.)

ILLUSTRATIONS.

(From Drawings by Mrs. A. I. McConnochie.)

BALLADS.

(The Text is edited and the Notes supplied by Mr. William Walker, Author of the "Bards of Bon-Accord".)

DISTANCE TABLE

DEESIDE SECTION

OF THE

GREAT NORTH OF SCOTLAND RAILWAY

(See also page 53)

	Cambus o' May	Dinnet	Aboyne	Dess	Lumphanan	Torphins	Glassel	Banchory	Crathes	Park	Drum	Culter	Milltimber	Murtle	Cults	Ruthrieston	Aberdeen
Ruthrieston																	2
Cults																1¾	3¾
Murtle															1¾	3½	5½
Milltimber														1¼	2¾	4¾	6½
Culter													1¼	2½	4	5¾	7¾
Drum												2¼	3¼	4½	6	8	9¾
Park											1	3¼	4¼	5½	7	9	10¾
Crathes										3¼	4¼	6¼	7½	8½	10¼	12	14
Banchory									3	6¼	7¼	9¼	10½	11½	13¼	15	17
Glassel								4½	7½	10¾	11¾	13¾	15	16	17¾	19½	21½
Torphins							2½	7	10	13	14	16¼	17¼	18½	20¼	22	23¾
Lumphanan						3	5½	10	13	16¼	17¼	19¼	20½	21½	23¼	25	27
Dess					2¾	5¾	8¼	12¾	15¾	19	20	22	23¼	24¼	26	27¾	29¾
Aboyne				2¾	5½	8½	11	15½	18½	21¾	22¾	24¾	26	27	28¾	30½	32½
Dinnet			4½	7¼	10	13	15½	20	23	26¼	27¼	29¼	30½	31½	33¼	35	37
Cambus o' May		2½	7	9¾	12½	15¾	18	22½	25½	28¾	29¾	31¾	33	34	35¾	37½	39½
Ballater	4	6½	11	13¾	16½	19½	22	26½	29½	32¾	33¾	35¾	37	38	39¾	41½	43½

Population, Churches, and Banks of Deeside Parishes, &c.

Parishes, &c.	Population.	Churches.	Banks.
Aboyne-Glentanner, ...	1403	E., F., Ep., R.C.	N. of S.
Ballater (Police Burgh), ...	985		N. of S., T. & C., U.
Banchory (,,), ...	1450		N. of S., T. & C., U.
Banchory-Devenick, ...	1981	E., F.	
Banchory-Ternan, ...	3193	E., F., U.P., Ep.	
Birse, ...	1154	E., R.C. ...	
Braemar (*quoad sacra*), ...	835	E., F., Ep., R.C.	U.
Coull, ...	746	E.	
Craigiebuckler (*quoad sacra*),	923	E.	
Crathie, ...	669	E., F.	
Dinnet (*quoad sacra*), ...	610	E.	
Drumoak, ...	869	E., F.	
Durris, ...	918	E., F.	
Echt, ...	1207	E., F.	T. & C.
Glengairn (*quoad sacra*), ...	414	E., F., R.C. ...	
Glenmuick and Tullich, ...	2299	E., F., Ep. ...	
Kincardine O'Neil, ...	1830	E., F., Ep. ...	
Logie-Coldstone, ...	938	E.	
Lumphanan, ...	992	E., F.	N. of S.
Maryculter, ...	1030	E., F., R.C. ...	
Nigg, ...	1572	E., F., Ep. ...	
Peterculter, ...	3629	E., F., Ep. ...	
Skene, ...	1673	E., F., Cong. ...	
Strachan, ...	655	E., F.	
Tarland, ...	736	E., F.	T. & C., U.
Torphins, (*quoad sacra*), ...	822	E., F.	T. & C.

Balmoral Castle.

DEESIDE.

I.—THE DEE.

'Mang silver birk and bracken green,
It winds and wimples owre ilk stane,
And laughs and gurgles soft and low,
As if 'twould stay its ebb and flow;
Then, rushing on with eager haste,
Unthinking of its waters' waste,
It flows out to the mighty sea,
Our ever rolling Royal Dee!

THE Aberdeenshire Dee is the most interesting and beautiful river in the Scottish Highlands. From its sources among the Cairngorm Mountains to where its sparkling waters pour into the North Sea at Aberdeen, not a single reach of its scenery lacks beauty or interest, while at many points its charms can hardly be surpassed. In these days of the commercial utilisation of our rivers it may be stated as a remarkable fact that its stream has not yet been employed to turn a single mill-wheel. Between Braemar and Aberdeen nearly every one of its affluents pays tribute to industry, but no such levy has ever been made on the main course of the river.

The valley of the Dee and the glens formed by

its numeroûs tributaries afford abundant and charming examples of nearly every variety of Highland scenic beauties. Richly wooded, gorgeous in their seasons with golden broom and whin and purple heath, the hills, as we lengthen our distance from the sea, increase in height, till we face the classic precipices of Lochnagar and the wild corries of the giant Cairngorms. The serene stillness of the little woodland loch of Aboyne gives place at higher altitudes to the sterner surroundings of Lochs Kinord and Davan, the lonely grandeur of Loch Muick, and the gloom of the Dubh Loch. The song of the waterfall is as common as the odour of the pine forests and the delightful fragrance of the birch woods and of the modest bog-myrtle. The ancient towers of Drum and Abergeldie, and the ruins of Birse and Knock, relics of feudal days, stand in striking contrast to the splendid modern palatial buildings of Balmoral, Invercauld, and Glentanner. Volumes have been written upon the domestic annals and legendary lore of the district and its ancient families. The moors and forests abound with game, and the streams with fish, and rare alpine plants flower upon the higher hills. Add to these glories its supreme advantages as a health resort, the possession of the purest and most bracing air in Britain, and one cannot wonder that the valley teems with visitors every summer and autumn. In annually increasing numbers they crowd every mansion, farm-house, and cot, from Bridge of Dee to Inverey. Tourists and sportsmen, cyclists and mountaineers, of every grade, from the prince of royal blood, who delights in deer-stalking, to the humblest city mechanic, who has to content himself with the trout-fishing or rambling of a single annual holiday, all appreciate the health and recreation to be found amid the ever varying attractions of Deeside.

While the Dee cannot claim the distinction of being either the longest* or the largest river in Scotland, it has the honour of being the most rapid. True, that superiority has long been claimed for the Spey; but if we look at the lower altitude of its source, and the many parts where its waters run still and deep for miles, it must yield in this respect to the Dee. No river in Scotland has such a volume of water cradled at so great a height as the Dee. The group of mountains where its head streams rise occupies the centre of Scotland, and is much superior in average height to, and of greater extent than, any other in the United Kingdom. High among the summits of the Cairngorm Mountains, in the parish of Crathie-Braemar, the sources of the Dee are to be found, at over 4000 feet above sea level. To three of these summits, Ben Muich Dhui (4296 feet)—second only to Ben Nevis among the mountains of the British Isles —Braeriach (4248 feet), and Cairn Toul (4241 feet), "the infant Dee" is indebted for its birth; and its upper watershed, embracing the entire breadth of the county of Aberdeen for many miles, is mountain-girt on the North, West, and South.

---

*The following list of Scottish rivers, with their length in miles and area of basin in square miles, is compiled from a recently published Blue Book:—

1. Clyde,	98·5	1488·0		6. Don,	80·5	515·7
2. Spey,	98·0	1153·5		7. Forth,	64·5	627·9
3. Tweed,	96·5	1680·6		8. Nith,	61·2	496·6
4. Tay,	93·2	2384·4		9. Deveron,	60·0	474·1
5. Dee,	85·2	817·2		10. Findhorn,	56·5	307·2

The main source of the Dee is on Braeriach, at the Wells of Dee, on a great gravelly plateau of disintegrated reddish granite, over 4000 feet in height—the largest plateau, at such an altitude, in the British Isles. Braeriach, in some respects the grandest of the Cairngorms, lies on the march between the counties of Inverness and Aberdeen, on the North side sending its waters to the Spey, on the South to the Dee. Between Braeriach and Cairn Toul is a great corrie, popularly known as the Garchary, down which hurry several streams known as the Garcharies, or the Garchary Burns. The largest of these is "the infant Dee", and will be found marked on the Ordnance Survey Maps as Allt a' Gharbh Choire (the burn of the rough corrie). It has two tributaries from the South, the lower from Lochan Uaine, a lochlet perched on the North shoulder of Cairn Toul, the upper from the corrie about a mile West of Lochan Uaine. The main stream of the Garchary, however, rises on Braeriach itself, practically in two streams. The smaller of these (unmarked in maps) rises a little below the summit cairn of Braeriach, and the larger on the East side of the Western cairn. The sources of the latter stream are springs in the gravel popularly known as "The Wells of Dee". Yet even beyond them water may occasionally be found in what are generally dry gravelly channels; and numerous "tear tracks" that augment the stream in rain storms will also be noticed. It is only, however, during part of summer and autumn that the "Wells" can be observed, as for the greater portion of the year a covering of snow lies on the plateau of Braeriach. The plateau is 2½ miles in length by about a mile in breadth, so that the gathering ground there for a perennial water supply is very considerable; indeed the granite *debris* acts as a sponge, and seems little affected by the summer's drought. The two Braeriach burns unite at an altitude of about 3950 feet, and topple over the Fuar Gharbh-chioire (the cold, rough corrie), forming a fall of 600 feet, conspicuous from Ben Muich Dhui and Cairn Toul, and observable from greater distances —notably from the summit of Lochnagar. Here in the corrie, even in the month of July, the young river frequently flows under a great archway of snow. Receiving the two tributaries on the right bank it continues its course—a series of cascades rather than the ordinary flow of a stream—till at the height of about 1980 feet it enters Glen Dee. Here, after an Eastward course of nearly three miles, it is joined by a shorter stream with a lesser volume, the Allt na Leirg Gruamaich (the burn of the gruesome pass), better known simply as the Larig Burn. The course of this latter stream is a series of rapids, its apparent source being several lochans (there are but two worthy of note) in the great hollow between Ben Muich Dhui and Braeriach. These lochans are the Pools of Dee, sometimes inaccurately called the "Wells". They lie at a height of about 2700 feet, and have been formed by the great mass of rock and *debris* that has fallen from the mountains forming the sides of the gorge. There is no visible connection between the line of Pools; the Larig Burn first appears gushing up through the stones some few yards below the lowermost Pool—at once a considerable mountain stream. The Pools are clear and pellucid, with stony bottoms that have the appearance of being artificially laid.

Their source is not very apparent, but it is doubtless underground. A few yards within the march with Inverness-shire a small stream may be observed rushing down the slope of Ben Muich Dhui. It is known among foresters as the March Burn, and probably feeds the Pools, but ere it reaches the level of the glen it disappears among the stones. About a mile below the Pools the Larig Burn receives its only tributary of note, the Allt a' Choire Mhoir (the burn of the big corrie), which rises a few yards North of the cairn of Ben Muich Dhui, and, after a course of about a mile, joins the Larig Burn at a height of 2299 feet, where it is crossed by the glen track.

The united stream of the Garchary and Larig Burns receives the name of Dee, but, in some old maps, that name is withheld till the Geusachan Burn, three miles further down the glen, pays its tribute to the young river. Three small streams, however, join it on the right, and one on the left bank before this point. The former descend from the Eastern face of Cairn Toul, the latter from the West side of Ben Muich Dhui. Besides these streams there are numerous dry channels that give a good account of themselves at certain seasons; and there are not a few deep gashes formed in the 1829 and previous "floods". The Geusachan Burn is a considerable rivulet, about four miles in length, which rises to the West of the cairn of Cairn Toul, having a short tributary from Lochan Suarach, near the Feshie watershed. It joins the Dee at the mouth of Glen Geusachan, having on the right Beinn Bhrotain (3797 feet), and on the left the Devil's Point (3303 feet), the latter a precipitous granite pinnacle on the South side of Cairn Toul.

Having thus described the birth of the Dee, and brought the young river to a point where it is admitted by all geographers that the name "Dee" should be applied, we need not here further trace its course That may properly be done in the ordinary way—beginning at the mouth, the best known part, and working upwards.

The Dee flows over a gravelly bed for most of its course, and consequently loses a considerable proportion of its waters by percolation, this accounting for the lower reaches of the river having a smaller volume than might be expected. Its tributaries seldom join it at right angles, but rather in an Easterly-inclined direction. The channel of the Dee, broad and capacious, occupies nearly the middle line of the area drained. The water is everywhere distinguished by its limpid clearness, on account of the small proportion flowing through peat moss. Referring to the velocity of the stream, and the thorough drainage of the valley, a distinguished naturalist has observed that there are few tracts in Scotland so destitute of lakes, pools, or stagnant water of any kind as the hollow of the basin of the Dee. The trees of natural growth in the Dee Valley are (according to Dr. Macgillivray), chiefly alder, birch, hazel, oak, willow, and bird-cherry; while the trees that have been introduced and planted to form woods and forests include the fir or pine, Norway spruce, silver fir, ash, and elm.

The Dee is now generally regarded as the Deva of Ptolemy, but the meaning of the word is still a matter of speculation. It flows through or along the following parishes:—Crathie-Braemar, Glen-muick-Tullich-Glengairn, Aboyne-Glentanner, Birse,

Kincardine O'Neil, Strachan, Banchory-Ternan, Durris, Drumoak, Maryculter, Peterculter, Banchory-Devenick, Nigg, and Aberdeen. The principal tributaries are:—on the North bank the Lui, Quoich, Feardar, Gairn, Tullich Burn, Tarland Burn, Canny Burn, and Culter Burn; and on the South bank the Geldie, Ey, Clunie, Garbh Allt, Gelder, Girnock, Muick, Tanner, Feugh, Sheeoch, and Crynoch.

The range of hills forming the watershed on its right bank was anciently called "The Mounth". The "passes" across this range were distinguished by different names, generally with the affix "Mounth". The most Westerly of these is the Tolmount, on the borders of the counties of Forfar and Aberdeen, at the watershed of Glen Doll and Glen Callater. Coming Eastward we have the White Mounth—the ancient name of Lochnagar; the Capel Mounth, between Glen Clova in Forfarshire and Glenmuick in Aberdeenshire; the Fir Mounth, sometimes simply called the Mounth or Mount Road, between Brechin and Ballater across Mount Keen; Cairn O' Mount, on the borders of the parishes of Fordoun and Strachan, of old one of the principal roads between South and North; the Slug Mounth from Stonehaven, by the West side of Cairn-mon-earn, to the Dee; and the Causey Mounth in the parish of Banchory-Devenick, on the road which formerly led from the South, through Sir Walter Scott's "Muir of Drumthwacket", to the Fords or to the Ferry of the Dee and so to Aberdeen. This ferry was a little below the present Wellington Suspension Bridge, and was the joint property latterly of the laird of Pitfodels and the Corporation of Aberdeen. The Causey Mounth road was so called because the line of road passed through a moss that required causewaying to render it passable. In the year 1380 Paul Crabb, tenant of the lands of Kincorth in Nigg, on the South side of the ferry, gave an annuity towards the maintenance of this ancient highway, and latterly the Corporation of Aberdeen was entitled by Act of Parliament to levy tolls for its repair and maintenance.

As a salmon stream the Dee takes the front rank among Scottish rivers. According to a recent report of the Fishery Board for Scotland, "the weight of the heaviest salmon taken by fixed engines was 56 pounds, and by rod 47 pounds. There are no obstructions by dams or cruives, but there are waterfalls on the Feugh and Lui [what about the Muick?], and the proprietors are being communicated with in order to their being opened up, which could be done by slight cutting and ladders. The spawning grounds above are good and extensive". It may be mentioned also that the number of salmon captured in a recent year in the Dee in the "water" belonging to the estate of Glen-tanner was about 1000, and in the "water" leased in connection with the Invercauld Arms Hotel, Braemar, 730. But there is little hope of salmon becoming so plentiful as to require special bargaining between Deeside masters and servants, as was once the case, when the latter declined to be fed on salmon oftener than *twice a week!* This, however, has been lately explained by the statement that the salmon which fell to the servants was not the fresh but the salted article.

Before the construction of the Deeside Railway the beauties of the valley were little known, and at the opening few believed the line would prove remunerative. The first turf was cut on the estate of Park, by Mrs. A. J. Kinloch, on 5th July, 1852, and the line was open for traffic—from Ferryhill Station to Banchory—on 7th September, 1853. Guild Street Station was opened next year, when the Deeside trains ran into it, and at that time there were only three passenger trains in each direction daily. The first turf of the extension from Banchory to Aboyne was cut by the Marchioness of Huntly at Rosehill, Aboyne, on 2nd October, 1857, and this portion of the line was opened on 2nd December, 1859. The first turf of the extension from Aboyne to Ballater was cut at Ballater on 7th September, 1865, by Mrs. Farquharson of Invercauld, and the line opened for traffic on 17th October, 1866. It was at one time proposed to extend the railway to Braemar, and a tramway was actually made from Ballater to Bridge of Gairn but was taken up. The Deeside Railway was at first worked by the Scottish Central Railway Company in connection with the Scottish Midland and Aberdeen Lines. It now forms a branch of the extensive system of the Great North of Scotland Railway, and has proved one of the most profitable and beneficial enterprises in the North.

II.—ABERDEEN.

My Silver City by the Sea,
  Thy white foot rests on golden sands;
A radiant robe encircles thee
  Of woody hills and garden lands.
I'll lift my cap and sing thy praise
  By silent Don and crystal Dee;
Oh, bravely gentle all thy days,
  Fair City by the Sea!

THE City of Aberdeen, a County, a Parish, and a Royal Burgh, the county town of Aberdeenshire, lies between the mouths of the rivers Dee and Don, a small portion only lying on the South side of the Dee. As recently enlarged, its boundaries include Old Aberdeen, Woodside, Torry, and Ruthrieston; the population being about 145,000, it is the fourth largest city in Scotland. The area of the burgh is 6694 acres, the *second* largest city area in Scotland; the valuation (including railways, waterworks and tramways), is £753,802; and the Police force numbers 165. The Town Council consists of 34 members, from whom are elected the Lord Provost and six Baillies, the Magistrates of the City. It returns two members to Parliament, and altogether is a place of very considerable importance, as well as of high antiquity.

Aberdeen is familiarly known as "Bon-Accord" from its ancient motto, and as the "Granite City" from being mainly built of a light grey variety of granite that has a permanently clean appearance, very pleasing to the eye. It lies in lat. 57° 9′ N., and long. 2° 6′ W., and is the chief town and seaport of Scotland North of Dundee.

The principal street is Union Street, extending from Castle Street—*the* square of the town—Southwestward to the Free Church College, where it forks, one branch, Holburn Street, leading Southward to Bridge of Dee, the other by Alford Place and Albyn Place to the Rubislaw district, the "West End" of the city. The Midmar, Echt, and Skene roads enter the town mainly by Albyn Place. Northward from Castle Street is King Street, of which the Peterhead and Ellon turnpike is a continuation, crossing the Don by a bridge near its mouth. Opposite King Street, Marischal Street leads down to the Harbour. A little West of King Street, Broad Street leads by Gallowgate and Spital to Old Aberdeen, and the ancient "Brig o' Balgownie," which crosses the Don a little above the modern bridge. Still further Westward from Castle Street is St. Nicholas Street, which, along with George Street, leads to Kittybrewster and Woodside by the Inverurie road. Opposite St. Nicholas Street is Market Street, leading along the upper end of the Harbour to Torry, crossing the Dee by Victoria Bridge. Still further Westward is the ravine of the Den Burn (now covered up) spanned by Union Bridge, a handsome structure, the only visible arch of which is of 132 feet span. The Great North of Scotland Railway runs North along this ravine, on the West side of which are Union Terrace Gardens, the Terrace leading to the Rosemount district. Opposite Union Terrace, Bridge Street leads to the

Railway Station. West of Bridge Street, Crown Street leads to the Ferryhill district, and, by the Wellington Suspension Bridge over the Dee, into Kincardineshire. Near its junction with Union Street, Crown Street is intersected by a continuation of Hardgate, the old entrance to the city from the South. A short distance along Holburn Street is Great Western Road, leading through Cuparstone and Mannofield to Cults by the North Deeside road.

The Mouth of the Dee.

The Dee enters the sea between the North Pier and the South Breakwater, works of considerable magnitude erected at different periods for the protection of the harbour entrance. North of the river's mouth a sandy beach stretches along the coast beyond the mouth of the Ythan, while on the South a rocky coast-line of gneiss with some granite intrusions extends for many miles. Torry Fort, formerly mounting nine guns, commands the entrance on the South side. A little further Eastward is Girdle Ness Lighthouse, built in 1833; it is open to visitors from 11 a.m. to 3 p.m., except on Saturdays and Sundays. The extreme height of the building is 131 feet; there are 189 steps, each rising seven inches. It is situated in lat. 57° 8′ N., and long. 2° 3′ W., off the sunken rock known as the Girdle, 25 miles from Buchan Ness Lighthouse and 43 from Bell Rock Lighthouse. The upper light is visible from the sea a distance of 19 nautical miles. Between Girdle Ness and Greg Ness, about three-quarters of a mile across, is the Bay of Nigg, an old debouchure, according to some authorities, of the Dee. Here at one time kelp and salt were made; and in 1804 the timbers of a ship were found in a field during the operation of drain-cutting. There has recently been erected here a Fish Hatchery and Laboratory in connection with the Fishery Board for Scotland. The ruins of St. Fittick's, the old parish church of Nigg, with the burial ground, are situated near the Bay. The church of Nigg was granted by William the Lion to the Abbey of Arbroath. The Caledonian Railway, after crossing the Dee by a viaduct between Wellington Bridge and Bridge of Dee, runs Eastward towards Greg Ness, thereafter holding Southward. A low ridge of hills, the Eastern extremity of the Grampians and the Mounth, ends at Greg Ness. Two "cairns" of this ridge are visible from Market Street—the one on the East called Baron's Cairn and the other Cat Cairn ("the Great and Small Laws" of fishermen). The latter is close to the turnpike leading South from Victoria and Wellington Bridges; the former was once known as the Cairn of Loirston. The church of Nigg, visible from so many points owing to its elevated situation, stands a little to the West of Cat Cairn on the opposite side of the road. It was built in 1829, at a cost of £1800, with a view to an expected increase of population on the erection of Wellington Bridge; but this expectation has not been realised in the direction anticipated. The Aberdeen prison overlooks the river on the South side, at Craiginches, a little South of Wellington Bridge.

On the North side of the mouth of the Dee is Footdee, the fishers' quarter, with several shipbuilding yards. Beyond are the "Links", with the Beach Battery, Gas Works, Swimming Baths, and Sea Bathing Station—the latter managed by the Corporation. The present channel of the Dee, below Wellington Bridge, was formed in 1869-72 in connection with certain Harbour improvements. The old channel was a little more to the North, and is partly utilised by the present Albert Dock, at the head of which is the Fish Market, one of the largest buildings of the kind in the country, best reached by Market Street. The ground in the neighbourhood is known as "The Inches", and is largely occupied by fishcuring establishments and timber yards and other premises, where a very great and constantly increasing business is carried on. The Harbour contains a Graving Dock and extensive Wet Dock accommodation.

At the East end of Castle Street is Castle Hill, surmounted by Barracks, whence a capital view may be had. In Castle Street stands the old Market Cross—

the finest in Scotland. It is hexagonal in form, w th carvings of the sovereigns of Scotland from James I. to James VII. From the top of the structure rises a tall, slender pillar surmounted by a unicorn of marble, supporting a scroll. A granite statue to "the fifth and last" Duke of Gordon is also worthy of notice. In Castle Street are also the fine buildings of the Salvation Army and the North of Scotland and Union Banks, but the principal structure is the Municipal Buildings. This last has a handsome clock tower, 190 feet high, from which one of the best views of the city may be had. Within the building is a statue of the Queen by the younger Brodie, a statue of Provost James Blaikie, by Sir John Steele, the reputed armour in which Provost Davidson fought at Harlaw, a fine painting of the late Prince Consort by Phillip, and many other objects of interest. The principal buildings in King Street are—on the East side—St. Andrew's (Episcopal) Cathedral, Central Fire Station, King Street School, and the Educational Trust Institution; on the West side—the Medical Hall, the North Parish Church, the East Poor House (in Nelson Street), and the Militia Barracks. Almost opposite the Poor House, on the East side of King Street, are Trinity Cemetery and the ancient Gallow Hill of the Burgh. Eastward from the latter, on the Links, is Broad Hill (94 feet). St. Peter's Cemetery is a little beyond the Militia Barracks.

Broad Street—sadly misnamed in these later days—gives entrance to Marischal College, where the Medical and Law Classes in connection with Aberdeen University are conducted. The present building of Marischal College was erected in 1837-41, and is a very handsome granite structure. Additions are in course of erection of a character so extensive and important that they will entirely alter its aspect and more than double its internal accommodation. The Mitchell Tower, occupying a position in the centre of the College, is remarkable for its height and beautiful proportions, and is already a noted landmark from considerable distances. The Gallowgate, with its narrow courts, one of the oldest and poorest parts of the city, is the old direct route to Old Aberdeen—an ancient, sleepy place containing two very interesting buildings, the Cathedral and King's College. All that remains of the Cathedral is the nave, still used as a church, and part of the transepts. Its twin towers and the graceful crown and lantern of crossed rib arches surmounting the tower of King's College are well known objects visible from many points. King's College was founded in 1494, and is mostly devoted to Arts and Divinity. It was united with Marischal College into one University in 1860.

St. Nicholas and George Streets are busy thoroughfares by which Old Aberdeen can also be reached, a divergence being made to the right near Kittybrewster station. At the East corner of Union and St. Nicholas Streets are the fine Roman classic building of the Town and County Bank, and a bronze statue of the Queen.

Market Street is one of the most important thoroughfares of the city. The harbour as well as the railway goods traffic mainly passes along it. Most passengers from the Railway station enter the city by it rather than by Bridge Street, notwithstanding the continual extension of the city Westward. It contains the Post Office (by and by to be removed to Crown Street) and the "New Market", the latter a fine large building near the upper end. It is 315 feet in length and 45 feet in height, and was built in 1840-42 at a cost of about £28,000. The Theatre, built in 1872, with accommodation for 1650 persons, stands in Guild Street, between Market Street and the Railway station.

Proceeding Westward, along Union Street, from the top of Market Street, the East and West Churches—the ancient Church of St. Nicholas—are passed on the right. They are surmounted by a tower (containing a peal of bells) and spire 200 feet high, and they are almost surrounded by the "Town's" Churchyard. Belmont Street joins Union Street at the East end of Union Bridge and leads to three important buildings in Schoolhill—Robert Gordon's College, the Art Gallery, and Gray's School of Art. In front of these buildings a statue has been erected by members of the Clan Gordon to the memory of the late General Gordon. Abutting Union Bridge, at the South-east corner, is Trinity Hall, the headquarters of the Seven Incorporated Trades of the City.

Crossing Union Bridge, on the right we reach Union Terrace with its public gardens and the handsome buildings of the Northern Assurance Company, the Grand Hotel, the Savings Bank, Parish Council Office, School Board Office, and Union Club. At the North end are the Public Library and the Free South Church, and beyond may be observed the Royal Infirmary, a plain but elegant building, its architectural beauties, owing to its position, being somewhat lost. Three statues adorn the Terrace—Prince Albert, Robert Burns, and Sir William Wallace, the last being of colossal proportions. The fine building of the Palace Hotel occupies the East corner of Union and Bridge Streets. The Music Hall, a large suite of buildings, with a portico of six Ionic columns, next attracts attention. A little beyond, Huntly Street, with the fine building of the Roman Catholic Cathedral, will be passed on the right.

Holburn Street is the principal entrance to the City from the South, the Dee being crossed by what is now known as the Old Bridge of Dee—for hundreds of years the only bridge that spanned the river in the vicinity of the city. The founder of the present structure was Bishop Elphinstone of Aberdeen, who died in 1514, a previous proposal (*c.* 1468) having come to nothing. His immediate successor does not appear to have interested himself very much in the matter; but Gavin Dunbar, the next Bishop, not only finished the building, but gifted the lands of Ardlair, in the parish of Kennethmont, for its maintenance. These lands were sold by the Town Council, on whom the care of the Bridge devolved, and the estate of Caprastone, Woodside, was purchased in 1610 with the proceeds. The bridge was originally only 16½ feet in width, but in 1842 was widened 11½ feet to the Westward by the Town Council, at a cost of over £7000. It has seven arches, with a total span of 432 feet. At its North-east end stood a chapel, dedicated to the Virgin Mary, containing an image of "Our Lady of Good Success", which had previously stood in one of the churches dedicated to St. Machar, before the erection of St. Machar Cathedral. In the early days of the Reformation the image was removed to Dunkirk, and thence to the Netherlands. In 1852 a chapel, Notre Dame de Finisterre, was specially built for its reception in Brussels. The Roman Catholics of Aberdeen have several times appealed for its restoration, but as yet unsuccessfully. There are, however, replicas in St. Peter's (Justice Street), and Blairs College. The last vestiges of a port and a watch-tower, erected at the South end of the bridge, where the citizens mounted guard in times of war and pestilence, were removed in 1773. In the beginning of last century the bridge had fallen into a state of decay, as a Latin inscription on a slab built into the West side testifies, the Town Council causing the whole of the arches to be rebuilt between the years 1719-23. The translation of another inscription reads: "Gavin Dunbar, Bishop of Aberdeen, caused me to be built over the river Dee, A.D. 1525". A sun-dial at the South-west end bears the date 1719, and at the North-east end a stone marks the height of the river on 6th August, 1829—the date of the great modern "Flood". "Masons' Marks" are numerous, and will interest the brethren of the mystic tie.

Two historic events took place at the bridge. In 1589 it was held by the forces of the Earl of Huntly, who fled before the Royal Army; and in 1639 Viscount Aboyne defended it against the Marquis of Montrose, but after two days' fighting the latter by a stratagem gained possession. "The Covenanters' Faulds" on the brae overlooking the South end of the bridge is believed to have been the camp of the victorious army, and the ballad at the end of this chapter celebrates the event.

Aberdeen has four public parks—the Victoria Park, Rosemount, near to which are the fine buildings of the Royal Lunatic Asylum; the Duthie Park (the gift of the late Miss Elizabeth Crombie Duthie) by the river side; the Stewart Park, Woodside; and the Union Terrace Gardens.

Tramways extend from Bridge of Dee, Mannofield, and Bayview (Rubislaw) to Union Street, and are continued to Bridge of Don *via* King Street. Kittybrewster and Woodside are connected with Union Street (top of Market Street); and there is a "circular route" to Rosemount by Union Terrace and Queen's Cross (West end of Albyn Place). A ride on the outside of a tramway car gives a capital idea of the town to a visitor who has but limited time at his command. A Bill is presently (1900) before Parliament for powers to construct additional tramways—to Ferryhill and the Sea Bathing Station.

The industries of Aberdeen are varied, and include beer, bricks, chemicals, combs, cotton, dressed granite, iron-founding, linen, meat and fish preserving, ropes, soap and candles, whiskey, woollen goods, ship-building, etc. But for all these, as well as many other particulars concerning the "braif toun" we must refer the visitor to Cadenhead's "New Book of Bon-Accord: a Guide to the City of Aberdeen".

BONNY JOHN SETON.

1. Upon the eighteenth day of June,
   A dreary day to see,
   The southern lords did pitch their camp
   Just at the bridge of Dee.

2. Bonny John Seton of Pitmeddin,
   A bold baron was he,
   He made his testament ere he went out,
   The wiser man was he.

3. He left his land to his young son,
   His lady her dowry,
   A thousand crowns to his daughter Jean,
   Yet on the nurse's knee.

4. Then out came his lady fair,
   A tear into her e'e;
   Says, Stay at home, my own good lord,
   O stay at home with me!

5. He looked over his left shoulder,
   Cried, Souldiers, follow me!
   O then she looked in his face,
   An angry woman was she:
   'God send me back my steed again,
   But ne'er let me see thee'!

6. His name was Major Middleton,
   That manned the bridge of Dee,
   His name was Colonel Henderson
   That let the cannons flee.

7. His name was Major Middleton
   That manned the bridge of Dee,
   And his name was Colonel Henderson
   That dung Pitmeddin in three.

8. Some rode on the black and grey,
   And some rode on the brown,
   But the bonny John Seton
   Lay gasping on the ground.

9. Then bye there comes a false Forbes,
   Was riding from Driminere;
   Says, Here there lies a proud Seton;
   This day they ride the rear.

10. Cragievar said to his men,
   'You may play on your shield;
   For the proudest Seton in all the lan'
   This day lies on the field'.

11. 'O spoil him! spoil him'! cried Craigievar,
'Him spoiled let me see;
For on my word', said Craigievar,
'He had no good will at me'.

12. They took from him his armour clear,
His sword, likewise his shield;
Yea, they have left him naked there,
Upon the open field.

13. The Highland men, they're clever men
At handling sword and shield,
But yet they are too naked men
To stay in battle field.

14. The Highland men are clever men
At handling sword and gun,
But yet they are too naked men
To bear the cannon's rung.

15. For a cannon's roar in a summer night
Is like thunder in the air;
There's not a man in Highland dress
Can face the cannon's fire.*

---

*The above is the earliest copy of the ballad which has come down to us, and first appeared in Maidment's "North Countrie Garland" 1824. The text is substantially the same as that which was given in "The Deeside Guide" (1832) by Joseph Robertson.

It was not Middleton (verses 6 and 7) but Lieut.-Col. Johnston who manned the bridge; Middleton was with Montrose. There is another version of the ballad given by Peter Buchan in "Ballads of the North of Scotland" which refers, in the usual style of traditionary ballad inaccuracy, to the contemplated burning of Aberdeen. The fright of the Highlanders at cannon, mentioned in the concluding verses (13-15), is noted in Gordon's "Scots Affairs" anent the Raid of Stonehaven, three days before the battle at Bridge of Dee.

III.—BRIDGE OF DEE TO BRIDGE OF FEUGH.

The burdens men have laid on thee,
  The tedium of the way
That thou hast travell'd night and day,
  Remember not—remember not,
To-night thou shalt be with the sea.

Tho' first there come an agony,
  For in the failing light
Thou hast to leave the land to-night,
  O fear it not—O fear it not,
Thou shalt be one, thou and the sea.

THE South end of the Bridge of Dee is in the parish of Nigg. The road Eastward leads to Torry and the Bay of Nigg; the Westward is the South Deeside road. The Stonehaven turnpike "takes the hill" at once so as to cross "The Mounth", and is joined a little beyond the fifth mile-stone (the tenth from Stonehaven) by the road from Wellington Bridge. The old South road, however, as may still be seen, kept by the river-side as far as the Burn of Leggart, over a quarter of a mile to the South-west, whence it took the high ground by Tollo Hill towards the "Causey Mounth". The Burn of Leggart divides the parishes of Nigg and Banchory-Devenick; and near its mouth, above the South Deeside road, has a short, narrow, picturesque "Den". The latter road crosses the burn at Hilldowntree, which was so named, according to tradition, from a tree that floated down the Dee, took root here, and grew to a gigantic size! The storm of 3rd October, 1860, overthrew this tree, but the root may still be seen. Public executions are believed to have taken place here in ancient times—a belief borne out by the name "Gallows Howe" in the vicinity.

Loirston Loch (269 feet) is about 1¾ miles South of the Bridge of Dee, and is drained by a small tributary of the Burn of Leggart. The Loch has gradually been reclaimed, its present extent being about 27 acres. The principal estates and proprietors in the Deeside portion of Nigg are:—Balnagask, Colonel James Davidson; Kincorth and Craigshaw, the Baker Incorporation of Aberdeen; Leggart, Sir David Stewart, LL.D.; and Redcraigs, Testamentary Trustees of the late John B. L. Birnie.

Blue Hill.

About a mile Westward from the Loch of Loirston stands Blue Hill (467 feet), on the estate of Banchory, on the South side of the road connecting Auchlunies with Nigg. It is interesting from its connection with the Ordnance Trigonometrical Survey and from the magnificent prospect that is to be had from its summit, recognisable at a distance by the flag-staff surmounting the cairn. In 1817 a base line (5 miles, 100 feet) was measured by chain on Belhelvie Links—an operation that took six weeks to perform—and the actual length was found to be only three inches less than the computed length. The latter length, founded on a base line measured by General Roy in 1784, on Hounslow Heath, was the computed length of the base of a triangle, the measured line on Belhelvie Links with extremities at Tarbathie and Leyton, the apex being the Blue Hill. The most distant points visible are Cairn Toul and

Beinn Bhrotain, on the borders of Inverness-shire, and Beinn a' Bhuird and Ben Avon on the borders of Banffshire. The following are also seen:—Cairn-mon-earn, Kerloch, Clochnaben, Mount Battock, Peter Hill, Mount Keen, Scolty, Lochnagar, Hill of Fare, Corrennie, Barmekin, Buck of the Cabrach, Tap o' Noth, Bennachie, and Brimmond Hill. Slains

The Blue Hill.

Castle is visible, as well as Buchan Ness Lighthouse, and the sea horizon is about 28 miles off. The most distant object seen in a Southerly direction is the Tower of Johnston, on Garvock Hill, near Laurencekirk. (See article and view, "The Blue Hill", by

Alexander Cruickshank, LL.D., and Alexander Copland, in Vol. I. of *The Cairngorm Club Journal).* The public are indebted to Sir David Stewart for the facilities afforded them of enjoying a view of almost phenomenal extent, and of these much advantage is taken.

Banchory House.

Banchory House is situated on the rising ground on the South side of the road between the third and fourth mile-stones. The present house was built in 1839, and is a charming residence, in the Elizabethan style, occupied by Sir David Stewart, LL.D., ex-Lord Provost of Aberdeen. The superiority of the lands of Banchory-Devenick, was granted by Alexander II., in 1244, to the Monks of Arbroath, who in 1256 gave a charter of them to Alan the Durward, who became Regent of Scotland. Alexander III. converted the lands into a "free barony", and conferred them on him as "the most accomplished knight and best military leader of his time". In 1333 they were held by William of Melgdrum, whose descendants, the Meldrums of Fyvie, retained them for over 200 years. In 1555 they came into the possession of George Gardyne. His grand-daughter Beatrix was a maid of honour to Queen Mary, who called her the "Queen of Song". Beatrix married Findla Mohr and so became the ancestress of the Clan Farquharson. In 1743 these lands were bought by Alexander Thomson, Advocate in Aberdeen, a descendant of John Knox, and in 1872 were sold to John Stewart, father of the present proprietor. The Prince Consort stayed at Banchory House while attending the meeting of the British Association at Aberdeen in 1859. A granite obelisk at Cotcraig on Tollo Hill bears the inscription: "In remembrance of the visit of H. R. H. Albert, Prince Consort, to this spot, xv. September, MDCCCLIX". Since then his son-in-law, the Marquis of Lorne (1898), now Duke of Argyll, Stanley, the great African traveller (1890), and many other distinguished men have been guests at Banchory House.

Banchory-Devenick.

The Church of Banchory-Devenick—a very plain building—was built in 1822 on the site of the previous edifice. It was anciently a prebend of St. Machar Cathedral, and was granted with the Kirk-lands to the See in 1163 by Malcolm IV. Devenick, the titular saint of the parish, was one of St. Columba's disciples. He was sent to Caithness-shire, in the seventh century, by his friend and co-worker St. Machar, and Barbour relates that the latter brought St. Devenick's body to Aberdeen and buried it in the churchyard of Banchory-Devenick. It was one of the last parish churches in the country where the Episcopal ritual was performed. In the churchyard may be seen an iron coffin-shaped chest which was used in "Resurrection" days to prevent the corpse being "lifted". The coffin was buried inside the iron chest, which was removed again after a few weeks.

It is interesting to note that Rev. George Skene Keith, D.D., famous for his *Agricultural Survey oj Aberdeenshire*, was schoolmaster here in 1771-8.

The Free Church was erected in 1844, and is situated, with a burial ground, in a small wood about half-a-mile to the South of the parish church.

About half-a-mile West of the parish church the Dee is crossed by St. Devenick Bridge, a neat suspension bridge for foot passengers, erected in 1837 by Rev. George Morison, D.D., the minister of the parish, at a cost of about £1400. The span between the main pillars is 185 feet. Previous to 1837 there was a "parish boat" for conveying worshippers across the river from the North (Cults) side of the parish (as then constituted) to the church. Locally the bridge is known as "Morison's Bridge", and the "Shakin' Briggie". The Dee makes a semicircular sweep here, the low-lying ground between the road and the river being known as the Haugh of Ardoe or Chalmers' Haugh.

Ardoe.

The estate of Ardoe (Alexander M. Ogston) is on the South side of the river, opposite St. Devenick Bridge. It was at one time divided into two portions, the "Sunny Half of Ardoe", and the "Shady Half of Ardoe", the latter lying about mid-way between the church of Banchory-Devenick and Ardoe House. The estate was purchased in 1744 for £700 by one Fordyce, who had been a "gunner's mate on board the *Centurion*, Lord Anson, on his voyage round the world". It is stated that Fordyce rode on horseback from London to Aberdeen with his prize-money in specie in his saddle-bags! At that time the estate was in such a wretched condition that the tenant of the then mansion house, with forty acres of land attached, refused a renewal of his lease at £5 a year (an increase of £1 13s. 4d. on the old rent), with the remark, "Na, by my faith, God has gi'en me mair wit"! In 1839 the estate was bought for about

£19,000, by the late Mr. Alexander Ogston, Aberdeen, whose son erected the present mansion house in 1878. The Burn of Ardoe, which enters the Dee West of Ardoe House, forms the boundary between Banchory-Devenick and Maryculter.

Heathcot adjoins Ardoe on the West; a little to the South of Heathcot is the old mansion house of Auchlunies; while in the immediate vicinity, to the West, is the mansion house of Shannaburn. The latter is situated on the left bank of a small stream called Shanna Burn; Heathcot lies between that burn and the Burn of Ardoe. At one time Shannaburn and Heathcot formed part of Auchlunies.

Blairs.

About three quarters of a mile West of Ardoe House, on the South side of the road, will be observed the Roman Catholic College of St. Mary's. The estate of Blairs, at one time the property of the Knights Templars, latterly belonged to the Menzies of Pitfodels, and was gifted in 1827 by John Menzies, the last of that old family, to the Church of Rome. Blairs College is an institution for the education of young men desirous of qualifying for the priesthood. The old mansion house of the estate, which, until recently, had served all the purposes of the College, having become totally inadequate to the demands of the present day, is giving place to a new college which is in course of erection. The first wing facing the West has already been completed, and is occupied by the Rector and Staff, and over eighty students. A very handsome church is nearly completed, and when the front wing is finished, uniting it to the existing wing, new Blairs will be one of the most striking buildings on

Deeside. The principal architectural features will be the college tower and the lofty church spire. The library contains about 15,000 volumes, many of them so valuable and rare that it has been described as a "priceless and unexplored field". Several Roman coins, found in the Red Moss of Crathes, are preserved here. Among the pictures in the College is an original portrait of Cardinal Beaton, and a remarkable portrait of Mary Queen of Scots in the dress worn by her on the scaffold. The latter is said to have been painted from a miniature given by the Queen herself to Elizabeth Curle, the maid of honour who was present at her execution.

The wood o' Kin'cousie is a' o'ergrown
Wi' mony a braw apple tree—
Sae will ye no leave the Gallowgate Port,
An' come to Kin'cousie wi' me?

Kingcausie.

The estate of Kingcausie is next entered, the mansion house, fully a mile Westward from Blairs College and seven miles from Aberdeen, being pleasantly situated among trees, on the South side of the road. Descendants of the family of Drum were long proprietors of the estate, but the male succession of the Irvines failed in the end of last century, A massive circular tower, on a prominent position on the hill of Auchlee, is erected in memory of John Irvine Boswell, of Balmuto and Kingcausie, who died in 1860. He was the only son of Claude Boswell, Advocate, Lord Balmuto, who in 1793 married Anne Irvine, the heiress of Kingcausie. A few yards West of the mansion house is the Corbie Linn, a beautiful waterfall on Crynoch Burn, which, separating the properties of Kingcausie and Maryculter, joins the Dee in the immediate vicinity. The turnpike crosses the burn by "Milton Bridge", at the West end of which is Mill Inn, an ancient and favourite halting place, a hostelry of some sort having existed here from time immemorial. A ferry was formerly the only means of communication with the North side of the river, but now a bridge of graceful design and elegant proportions gives access to Milltimber station. It has five spans—one central span of 94 feet clear waterway, two side spans of 54 feet clear waterway each, and two masonry side arches, each of 15 feet span, giving in all a clear waterway of 232 feet. There are two piers in the river, built of masonry and founded at a depth of 9 feet below the bottom of the river. The erection of this bridge will popularise still further the drive from Aberdeen to Mill Inn—an old favourite with excursionists. The Mill of Maryculter Friendly Society was established in 1830; it met and dined at least once a year, and included many gentlemen of social position. Special rooms were at one time reserved at the Mill Inn for its meetings, but it was by no means confined to one meeting-place. The last dinner was eaten at Alford in 1859.

Maryculter.

Maryculter House and the ruins of the old church are about a mile West from Mill Inn, along a pleasant, tree-lined drive, during which we pass the Insch of Culter, a considerable stretch of level land bounded on the North, but formerly on the South, by the Dee. The diversion, it is generally believed, happened over three hundred years ago. The greater part of the parish was granted in the end of the twelfth century to the Knights Templars, who were succeeded by the Knights of St. John of Jerusalem. The Menzies of Pitfodels acquired considerable portions of the Templar lands between 1528 and 1618, and the mansion house was probably built about the latter date. The ruins of the old church, with the churchyard, are close to the mansion house. Some five hundred years ago the Knights Templars were owners of fully 8000 acres of land in Maryculter and Peterculter. Down by the river, where the house of Maryculter now stands, they had their preceptory. They had several churches, and, in Maryculter particularly, there may still be found March Stones with Maltese Crosses cut on them. In the churchyard, there lay, till recently, two very fine stone effigies, representative of two members of the Menzies family; they are now resting on the sills of two of the windows of the West Kirk in Aberdeen. The new church, built in 1782, is on the South side of the road, about a mile from the old site. In the burying ground attached to it is a tombstone to the memory of Rev. John Bower, a minister of the parish, who died in 1866. His father was a teacher in Aberdeen, and it was his school in Longacre that Lord Byron first attended. The poet thus writes of the circumstance:—"I was sent at five years old, or earlier, to a school kept by a Mr. Bowers, who was called 'Bodsy Bowers' by reason of his dapperness. It was a school kept for both sexes. I learned little there. . . ."

A direct road from Stonehaven joins the Deeside road a few yards short of the eighth mile-stone, and almost opposite Maryculter House. A mile farther Westward is Altries House.

The estates and proprietors in the parish of Maryculter are:—Altries, Trustees of the late A. J. Kinloch; Auchlunies, Testamentary Trustees of the late Peter Duguid; Blairs, Archbishop Eyre and others; Heathcot, Alexander M. Ogston; King-causie, Mr. and Mrs. Irvine Fortescue; Maryculter, Sir Cosmo E. D. Gordon, Bart.; and Shannaburn, Mrs. Fergusson.

Where the birk tree like silver is shining,
And the broom on the brae gleams like gold.

Durris.

The parish of Durris (of old *Dores*, as it is still locally pronounced) is entered at a point due South from the ruined church of Drumoak. Just beyond the eleventh mile-stone a road branches off on the right towards Park Bridge over the Dee. This bridge is private property, having been erected by the railway company, and a small toll is accordingly exacted. At the South-east end of the bridge is a small eminence surmounted by an octagonal tower, about 80 feet in height. The estate of Durris—which practically comprehends the whole parish, with a slice of Banchory-Ternan—at one time belonged to the Earl of Peterborough (passing from the Frasers by marriage), and came into possession of the Duke of Gordon as next heir of entail, after a protracted law suit. The Duke erected the tower to commemorate his legal victory, contenting himself with the simple inscription of the date, 1825, which doubtless at the time was considered sufficient to indicate its *raison d'etre* to future generations. There is an inside stair-case with 62 steps. Keith's Pot and Keith's Stone, just below Park Bridge, derive their names, according to tradition, from a romantic story. Ignoring a family feud, a young Keith loved one of the ladies of Drum, who was nothing loth. Surprised during one of their stolen meetings, young Keith fled and swam for the South bank of the Dee, and, resting on a stone in the centre of the river, was shot by his pursuers. Eastward of the Duke's Tower is a Market Stance, where a fair was till recently held, probably representing St. Congal's Fair, anciently held "at the kirk of Doors in Mernshire". The Tower and the Stance are within a bend of the river known as Kincluny, which has also an eminence called Gallow Hill.

Durris House is about a mile South from the Tower and is pleasantly situated, with a romantic "Den" at the back. The policies are unique in respect to the number, variety, and size of the ornamental trees and shrubs. Almost every known species of pine is represented, and there are also specimens of rare and beautiful elms, ashes, beeches, sycamores, and planes. The "Nobilis" Avenue (*Pinus Nobilis*) is particularly worthy of notice. Professor Cosmo Innes was born at Durris House in 1798. Durris was granted by the Bruce to William Fraser, second son of his brother-in-law, Sir Alexander Fraser. In 1834 the estate was sold by the Duke of Gordon to Anthony Mactier, formerly of Calcutta, but a native of Galloway. His son sold it for £300,000 in 1871 to Dr. James Young, of paraffin fame, who died in 1883. In 1890 the estate was purchased by Mr. Henry Robert Baird. On the north side of the road, near Kirkton, is a small hillock known as Castle Hill. Here, when the lands were mostly forest, the kings of Scotland had a hunting-seat, which must have been a place of some strength, as formerly evidence was not altogether wanting that it had been protected by artillery. It is believed that in the reign of Alexander III. a bridge crossed the Dee here.

The church and Kirkton of Durris are about 14 miles from Aberdeen, on the Burn of Sheeoch, which, rising on the East side of Kerloch, has a somewhat picturesque course of nearly 12 miles. The church, which is concealed from view by trees, was originally a rectory in the Diocese of St. Andrews. The bell bears the inscription: "Iohn Mowat, Old Abd. Fe. 1765; in usum ecclesiæ de Durris. Sabata Pango, Funera Plango". The burial aisle of the original Frasers of Durris is at the East end of the church; the oldest inscribed date is 1587. The Free Church is near the left bank of the Sheeoch, about three quarters of a mile South-west of Kirkton. There is no prettier spot on lower Deeside more heedlessly passed by than Durris at the Bridge of Sheeoch, where the road is carried over the stream. The bridge has an elegant arch, and the dell has quite a romantic appearance.

The parish is connected with the North side of the river by two bridges, Park Bridge (already referred to) and Durris Bridge, about a mile and a half West of Kirkton. The latter was erected in 1862 by the then proprietor of Durris, and is within half a mile of Crathes station. The "Slug Road" from Stonehaven intersects the parish, crossing the Mounth between Cairn-mon-earn (1245 feet) and Craig Beg (1054 feet). The hill range to the Eastward is of considerably lower elevation than Cairn-mon-earn; viewed from it, the Eastern hills are rather insignificant. There is a fine view from the summit, which is surmounted by a natural cairn about 65 yards in circumference, with an artificial cairn in the centre. Immediately to the North, and separated by a slight depression, is Mount Dernal (1100 feet), rather flat topped, and from some points of view indistinguishable from Cairn-mon-earn. Craig Beg is a mile South-westward from Cairn-mon-earn, and is surmounted by two small cairns. From the North side of the Dee the contour of these two hills is very pleasing. Mongour (1232 feet) is a mile South-westward of Craig Beg, and has a chalybeate spring known as Red Beard's Well. There is a cave on Craig Beg where, according to tradition, a band of robbers, headed by one "Red Beard", lay in wait for travellers. The robber-chief has left his name to both well and cave. On the left bank of the Burn of Sheeoch is a height named Cairn Shee (725 feet), about a mile and a half South-westward from Durris Bridge. Among other benefactions to the parish, Alexander Hogg, a native, left ten shillings yearly to the herds round this hill, for the purpose of making a midsummer fire on it, in remembrance of the fact that he had once herded cattle there. The herds, in the persons of the youngest male servants, each receive sixpence at sun-down on 24th June, and the onlookers are treated to bread, cheese, and ale; the function has now (1900) taken place 112 times.

"The famous Mr. Davidson"—who expiated his crimes on the scaffold—among his other robberies stole "Ye Presbytrie Buik of Aberdeen begun ye 20 day of October, 1598, and continued to 14 June,

1610", from the manse of Durris on 28th February, 1747. The volume fell into the possession of the Faculty of Advocates, who, in 1891, returned it to the proper owners.

We enter the parish of Banchory-Ternan a mile West of Durris Bridge, and in about two miles farther on reach the Feugh—18 miles from Aberdeen and 17 from Fettercairn. Just before reaching Bridge of Feugh two islets will be observed formed by the Dee.

Coaching parties from Aberdeen to Banchory generally drive up the North road, and return by the South, thus obtaining excellent views of both sides of the Dee. The round may be shortened as circumstances require by crossing the river at Maryculter, Park, or Durris.

LIZZIE LINDSAY.

1. 'Will ye gang to the Highlands, Lizzie Lindsay?
 Will ye gang to the Highlands wi me?
 Will ye gang to the Highlands, Lizzie Lindsay?
 My bride an my darling to be'?

2. She turned her round on her heel,
 And a very loud laugh gaed she:
 'I'd like to ken whaur I'm ganging
 An wha I am gaun to gang wi'.

3. 'My name is Donald Macdonald,
 I'll never think shame or deny;
 My father he is an old shepherd,
 My mither she is an old dey'.

4. 'Will ye gang to the Highlands, bonnie Lizzie?
 Will ye gang to the Highlands wi me?
 For ye shall get a bed o green rashes,
 A pillow an a covering o grey'.

5. Upraise then the bonny young lady,
An drew till her stockings an sheen,
An packd up her claise in fine bundles,
An away wi young Donald she's gaen.

6. When they cam near the end o their journey,
To the house o his father's milk-dey,
He said, Stay still there, Lizzie Lindsay,
Till I tell my mither o thee.

7. 'Now mak us a supper, dear mither,
The best o yer curds an green whey,
An mak up a bed o green rashes,
A pillow an covering o grey'.

8. 'Rise up, rise up, Lizzie Lindsay,
Ye have lain oer lang i the day;
Ye should hae been helping my mither
To milk her ewes an her kye'.

9. Out then spak the bonnie young lady,
As the saut tears drapt frae her ee,
'I wish I had bidden at hame,
I can neither milk ewes nor kye'.

10. 'Rise up, rise up, Lizzie Lindsay,
There is mair ferlies to spy;
For yonder's the Castle o Kingussie,
An it stands high an dry'.

11. 'Ye are welcome here, Lizzie Lindsay,
The flower o all your kin,
For ye shall be lady o Kingussie,
An ye shall get Donald my son'.*

---

*From the singing of George Mitchell, ground officer at Edzell Castle (5 Oct., 1891), as learned by him, fifty-eight years before, from his step-grandmother, Nellie Low, she being at that time 80 years old, and having learned it from singers in her girlhood.

Seven traditionary versions of this ballad (exclusive of the above) are given in Child's "English and Scottish Popular Ballads", along with a number of minor variations, and almost all of them give the hero as the heir of Kingcausie. According to tradition the heroine is said to have been a daughter of Lindsay of Edzell, but no historical confirmation has been obtained connecting it either with the Kingcausie or the Edzell families.

First mentioned in Johnson's "Musical Museum" (No. 434) where Burns contributed the air along with the first stanza. Robert Allan added two stanzas to this in R. A. Smith's "Scottish Minstrel" (vol. ii., p. 100), making Lizzie a poor lassie. In 1805, Professor Scott of Aberdeen sent a copy (fragmentary) of the ballad to Jamieson, which was printed in his "Popular Ballads", 1806 (vol ii., p. 149), with corrections from the editor's recollection. Two versions are in the Kinloch MSS., one of which is printed in Aytoun's "Ballads of Scotland" (vol. i., p. 277). Buchan prints the ballad in what he calls "its complete state, for the first time" in "Ballads of the North of Scotland", 1828 (vol. ii., p. 102).

Music—Johnson, No. 434; Smith, ii., pp. 100-101; Graham, ii., p. 82; Christie, ii., p. 88; Privately Printed, Brighton, 1895; and Child, v., 421.

IV.—ABERDEEN TO CULTER.

Begone, away each gloomy care,
The sweets of nature let us share;
And hark the sound so full of joy,
And view the scenes that never cloy,
The peerless scenes, priceless and free,
Along the bonny banks of Dee.

MOST visitors to Deeside naturally avail themselves of the facilities afforded by the railway, the journey by which from Aberdeen to Ballater is described by four stages. The district comprised in this, the first, stage may be considered as part of the suburbs of the city of Aberdeen, the villas of the wealthier citizens dotting the whole distance, particularly on the North side of the line. In 1894 the railway company instituted a "Suburban Service" between Aberdeen and Culter. The stations and distances are:

Miles.		Miles.	
...	Aberdeen.	4⅛	West Cults.
1⅜	Holburn Street.	4¾	Bieldside.
1¾	Ruthrieston.	5⅜	Murtle.
3	Pitfodels.	6¼	Milltimber.
3⅝	Cults.	7⅜	Culter.

Holburn Street station is at the point where that street is crossed by the line, and is convenient for Duthie Park, Allenvale Cemetery, and Bridge of Dee.

Ruthrieston.

Ruthrieston station is close to the old Kaimhill road, and serves the Ruthrieston and Mannofield districts. In this neighbourhood, on Kaim Hill, stood the noted "Twa Mile Cross" of Aberdeen, not a trace of which remains. The site is generally believed to have been immediately South of the Mannofield Reservoirs, where a rough cairn, with a particularly large stone, said to be Druidical, may possibly mark the spot. Montrose here encamped in 1644 before the battle of the Justice Mills, in which he defeated the Covenanters, and then pillaged Aberdeen. The North Deeside road, from Great Western Road, runs parallel to the railway, and generally not far from the line. At Mannofield a road, branching to the right, leads to Countesswells and the Skene turnpike. In this vicinity are the lower Reservoirs in connection with the Aberdeen Water-works; they are situated at a height of 161 feet, and contain 18,000,000 gallons—about three days' supply. The old Deeside road is on the South side of the railway. Leaving Holburn Street at Bridge of Dee it keeps near the left bank of the river, and, crossing Kaim Hill, proceeds to the Burn of Cults at St. Devenick Bridge.

> The braif ald Baron is layd in graif,
> Jesu be praisit that his saul beis saif!
> Na haly priest leint our his hede,
> To schrive his sinnis on ane dying bed,
> Na beids were tauld, na bell was rung,
> Na haly messe was our him sung,
> But Sanct Devenick heard the piercing prayir
> That he raisit to heivin in his bitter dispayr,
> And gained it ane blissit welcum thair.

Pitfodels.

Pitfodels station perpetuates the name of one of the oldest residential estates near Aberdeen, which extended along the North side of the river from near Bridge of Dee to the Burn of Cults, and was possessed for nearly four hundred years by a branch of the Athole family of Menzies. The Lairds, the last of whom died in 1843, were noted for their adherence to the Roman Catholic religion, and to the ancient royal family of Scotland.

> Gilbert Menzies of Pitfodels
> Did for King Charles wear the blue.

In 1745, Gilbert Menzies, the then proprietor, raised a detachment of soldiers in aid of the Pretender. The ancient castle of Pitfodels stood at Castle-heugh, close to the river-side, within the present grounds of Norwood Hall. The whole estate has been divided into feuing plots for villas. A portrait of Provost Reid of Pitfodels, which hung in the Kirk Session-house of Aberdeen, was removed in 1640, because it offended certain "sojeris as smelling somequhat of poperie"!

Cults.

So many villas and cottages have been erected at Cults by citizens of Bon-Accord, that it now forms quite a large village, with two stations, Cults and West Cults. Cults is beautifully situated on high ground overlooking the valley of the Dee, with a fine southerly exposure, well protected from North winds by still higher ground behind. A steam pump in connection with the Aberdeen Water-works stands on the North side of the village; there is also an engine at the North end of St. Devenick Bridge for pumping water to the Pitfodels Reservoir. The estate of Cults formerly belonged to a branch of the Irvines of Drum.

Murtle.

The barony of Murtle anciently belonged to the Bishopric of Aberdeen. The mansion house, an elegant building in the Grecian style of architecture, is prettily situated on the South side of the railway. A short distance North from the station is the Den of Murtle, a picturesque and beautifully wooded little ravine, containing two small artificial lakes, which serve as dams for storing water for the corn mills below. The Den is crossed by the aqueduct of the Aberdeen Water-works; at the East side is Dalhibity, and on the West, Binghill; at the latter place there is a stone circle, and also a cairn, reputed by some, with but little reason, to have been an ancient burial place of the Irvines. About half a mile from the station, on the North side of the road is the Deeside Hydropathic Establishment, a large and imposing building containing about 100 bedrooms. Situated at an elevation of 350 feet above sea level it commands an extensive view of lower Deeside; the lakes in the Den near by, have been stocked with Loch Leven trout for the use of visitors. On the summit of Beans Hill (450 feet), a little to the West of the head of the Den, is the Weather or Wedder Craig, where there is a "Cupstone" known also as the "Doupin' Stane", on which the youngest burgess of Aberdeen present at the riding of the marches was wont to undergo a ceremony now falling into desuetude. The "official" "Doupin' Stane" is, however, on the farm of Wineford, Brimmond Hill, near the 31st March Stone. In 1707 the proprietor of Culter obtained the authority of an Act of Parliament for holding fairs on the muir here "for all kinds of vendible commodities".

Milltimber.

Milltimber is the nearest station to Mill Inn, Maryculter. Glasterberry, an experimental farm in connection with the researches of Mr. Thomas Jamieson, late Lecturer on Agriculture in Aberdeen University, lies a short distance Eastward, to the left of the road. Camphill, a modern house South-west of the station, takes its name from the neighbouring site of an ancient camp.

> Like silver shines the dimpling Dee,
> That seeks with rapid speed the sea.

Culter.

The village of Culter is about 8 miles from Aberdeen, and practically owes its existence to its celebrated paper works. The terminus of the Suburban line, Culter, besides being a place of no small business importance, is rapidly becoming a holiday resort, fully warranting its creation into a "Special Water and Drainage District" and the recent erection of the Gordon Arms Hotel. The first mill for the manufacture of paper by machinery in Scotland was erected here in 1750 by Bartholemew Smith, a Manxman, who had been "out in the '45". He announced his new venture in the *Aberdeen Journal* of 8th January, 1751; his staff consisted of six men, and he was wont to repair to Castle Street of Aberdeen on Fridays to buy "rags of all kinds of flax or hemp by the stone-weight" for his raw material. The paper works are on the South side of the road, immediately below the bridge spanning Culter Burn. They have passed through various hands, and are now owned by the Culter Mills Paper Company, Limited, with a capital of £70,000. The mills are connected with Culter station by a siding, and have a weekly output of over 100 tons, employing about 500 hands. Just above the bridge is the picturesque Den of Culter, which has been utilised as a reservoir for the water driving the mills. A wooden statue, intended to represent Rob Roy, has been placed by the villagers on the East side of the gorge.

Immediately below the paper works the rocky course of the burn is crossed by an old bridge in connection with the old North Deeside road. At one time there was a saw-mill near the mouth of the burn, to which, till about 1750, trees were floated down from the upper reaches of the Dee. Formerly there was also a snuff manufactory here. The corn mill of Kennerty is situated between the railway and the paper works. The Burn of Culter is formed by the junction of two small streams; the easterly is the Leuchar Burn from the Loch of Skene, the westerly the Gormack Burn from the Hill of Fare. Just above its junction with the Gormack, the Leuchar is crossed by a bridge which was built in 1608, and repaired in 1710, as the dates inscribed testify. Near the bridge, says *The Statistical Account*, "are the remains of a rampart called the guard-dike. Tradition informs that a strong guard of armed men was stationed here to prevent all communication between the sound and the infected, while the plague raged in Aberdeen and its environs, about 130 years ago".

The church of Peterculter, surrounded by patriarchal trees, lies in the lower angle formed by the confluence of the Burn of Culter with the Dee, is built on the site of an ancient chapel dedicated to St. Peter. St. Peter's Well, at one time noted for the qualities of its water, is on the Glebe Haugh, a short distance Eastward from the church. Peter's Heugh is the name of the adjoining part of the left bank of the river. The present church was erected in 1779, its immediate predecessor having been built after 16th October, 1673, on which date the former church fell to the ground. A new Free Church has been built in the village; the old one stood on the southern base of Beans Hill.

Culter House, at one time described as "one of the most beautiful and best finished gentlemen's seats in the North", is almost opposite Camphill. In front is a fine avenue of trees known as the Lovers' Walk, while behind are the Bride's Ward and the Bride's Well. A considerable part of the estate of Culter belonged in early times to the Knights Templars, and afterwards to Alan the Durward, but in 1247 it became the property, by royal grant, of the Allans of Wauchop, from whom it descended by marriage to the Cumins of Inverallochy. The oldest part of the house is said to have been built by the Sir Alexander Cumming of Queen Mary's time, "a very extravagant and haughty knight, who had his horse shod, at the Queen's wedding, with silver shoes, so lightly fastened on that, when the animal caracoled, they fell off to be picked up by the mob". His coat of arms, much weather worn, may still be seen in front of the house. The now extinct baronetcy of Cumming of Culter was created in 1672. In 1726 Sir Alexander Cumming sold the estate to Patrick Duff of Premnay, who married Margaret, only daughter of Duff of Braco, when she was but eleven years of age.

The estates and proprietors in Peterculter, exclusive of the Cults division, are: Culter (part of) Robert William Duff; and Drum Schivas, Mrs. Irvine (as curatrix for Alexander Forbes Irvine).

Normandikes.

About a mile South-westward from the church of Peterculter, on rising ground between the railway and the river, is one of the greatest antiquarian curiosities on Deeside—the remains of a Roman Camp, locally known as Normandikes. It may be observed from the train soon after leaving Culter, and is held by some to mark the site of the Roman Devana, while others contend that Loch Davan at Dinnet is better entitled to that honour. It lies immediately to the West of Alton, and a well on the eastern rampart is still known as Norman's Well or the Roman Well. A supposed "Roman Ford" across the Dee is still pointed out. The Camp is of an oblong rectangular form, the northern enclosing wall, which can be distinctly traced, being 985 yards in length. Authorities competent to deal with such questions express the belief that it was the work of Lollius Urbicus, who has been described as "the gallant Lieutenant of Antoninus", a Roman Emperor who died A.D. 161. It is a spacious enclosure, now planted with wood, capable of lodging a large army.

> 'Tis said, when nights are eerie,
>   When wind drives from the North,
> A sobbing and a wailing,
>   Out on the loch break forth.

Skene.

This parish has direct communication with Aberdeen by means of the "Skene" road, which forks some six miles from the city, one branch making for Strathdon, the other for Tarland. The Loch of Skene, which has an area of 312 acres, is about nine miles from Aberdeen, and is three miles in circumference, the greatest depth being about twelve feet. It was formerly visited by wild ducks, geese, and even swans, and is still noted for its pike. A canal was at one time projected from the loch to Aberdeen. The earliest recorded proprietor of Skene is Alan the Durward. Robert Skene received a charter, still preserved, of the lands and Loch of Skene, from Robert the Bruce, in 1317. It remained, by the male line, in the Skene family till 1827, when it passed, through the female line, to the trustees of the Earl of Fife. The house of Skene was said to be "the first built stone house in Mar". Its walls were no less than ten feet in thickness, and for greater safety the second storey was entered by means of a ladder, while the third was "covered with a mount of earth", in which state the building remained till 1680. On the estate of Easter Skene, near the march with the parish of Kinellar, is a boulder with the inscription: "DRUM STONE. 1411. HARLAW". Here, says tradition, Sir Alexander Irvine of Drum rested and made his will while on his way to the battle of Harlaw—"the wiser man was he". The late Mr. William McCombie of Easter Skene was responsible for the inscription, which was cut in 1835; the stone was underbuilt and surrounded with a dwarf wall by the present proprietor in 1892.

The estates and proprietors in the parish are: Skene, Trustees of the late George Hamilton; Easter Skene, Peter D. McCombie; Hill Cairnie, Society of Advocates in Aberdeen; Leddach, Representatives of Douglas Gordon, and Mrs. Mather; Kirkville, Trustees of the late James Proctor—on this estate is Proctor's Orphanage; Easter Kinmundy and Fiddie, Trustees of the late Lieut.-Col. Henry Erskine Forbes; Brodiach, Dr. James E. Fowler; Westhill, Rev. W. M. Farquhar; Concraig, University of Aberdeen; Easter Carnie, the Dean of Guild of the Burgh of Aberdeen; Tertowie (part of), James A. G. King; and Garlogie Mills (woollen), Alexander Hadden & Sons. A direction post near the mills gives the following distances: Cullerlie, 1¾ miles; Raemoir, 8 miles; Torphins, 12 miles; Kincardine O'Neil, 13¾ miles; Lumphanan, 15 miles; Echt, 2¾ miles; Midmar, 5 miles; Cross Roads, 14½ miles; Tarland, 20½ miles. "Mason Lodge", at Leddach, derives its name from a lodge of freemasons, now extinct, which was established there in 1830.

Echt.

The principal topographical feature of Echt is the Hill of Fare, which is prominent from many points along Deeside. It is a long flattish hill, but from the South has rather a striking contour, the highest point (1545 feet) being towards the Western extremity. A little Eastward of the summit the battle of Corrichie was fought on 28th October, 1562. The opposing armies were headed respectively by the Earl of Huntly and the Earl of Moray. Huntly had taken the field against Queen Mary, but was thoroughly defeated. The Queen is said to have afterwards viewed the scene of the battle from a rock still known as the "Queen's Chair". "Queen Mary's Well" is also pointed out between the site of the battle and the "Chair".

Another interesting topographical feature is the Barmekin, a hill rising to the height of 899 feet, on the summit of which is a well-defined ancient camp or fortification of circular form, embracing no fewer than five entrenchments and rampart walls, within an area of about six acres. The interior enclosure is level, with a diameter of about 300 feet. Tradition is silent as to the origin of the camp, but it is generally supposed to be Caledonian. From the summit there is a capital view, including Kerloch, Clochnaben, Mount Battock, Lochnagar, and Bennachie, as well as the Lochs of Skene and Drum.

The principal mansion in the parish is Dunecht House, a magnificent building in the Grecian style of architecture, with a private chapel. Till recently it had an excellent observatory, which contributed not a little to the advancement of astronomical science. In 1881 the body of the 25th Earl of Crawford and Balcarres (to which family the estate then belonged) was stolen from the vault of the chapel, and the event naturally caused a profound sensation. Mr. Alexander Charles Pirie ownes the estates of Echt and Monecht, which embrace the greater part of the parish; Lieut-Col. F. N. Innes owns Cullerlie, and a small part of the estate of Skene is in the parish.

A finger-post at the village gives the following distances: Drum, 6½ miles; Banchory, 7½ miles; Raemoir, 6½ miles; Torphins, 11 miles; Dunecht, 2 miles; Waterton, 2¾ miles; Castle Fraser, 5¾ miles; Kintore, 8¼ miles.

The Battle of CORICHIE *on the* HILL OF FAIR.
Fought October 28, 1562.

1. Murn ye heighlands, and murn ye leighlands,
I trow ye hae meikle need;
For thi bonny burn o' Corichie
His run this day wi' bleid.

2. Thi hopefu' laird o' Finliter,
   Erle Huntly's gallant son,
For thi love hi bare our beauteous quine
   His gar't fair Scotland mone.

3. Hi his braken his ward in Aberdene,
   Throu dreid o' thi fause Murry;
And his gather't the gentle Gordone clan
   An' his father auld Huntly.

4. Fain wid he tak our bonny guide quine,
   An' beare hir awa wi' him;
But Murry's slee wyles spoil't a thi sport,
   An' reft him o' lyfe and lim.

5. Murry gar't rayse thi tardy Merns men,
   An' Angis, an' mony ane mair;
Erle Morton, and the Byres lord Linsay,
   An' campit at thi hill o' Fare.

6. Erle Huntlie came wi' Haddo Gordone,
   An' countit ane thusan men;
But Murry had abien twal hunder,
   Wi' sax score horsemen and ten.

7. They soundit thi bougills an' the trumpits,
   An' marchit on in brave array;
Till the spiers an' the axis forgatherit,
   An' than did begin thi fray.

8. Thi Gordones sae fercelie did fecht it,
   Withouten terrer or dreid,
That mony o' Murry's men lay gaspin,
   An' dyit thi grund wi' theire bleid.

9. Then fause Murry feingit to flee them,
   An' they pursuit at his backe,
Whan thi haf o' the Gordones desertit,
   An' turnit wi Murry in a crack.

10. Wi hether i' thir bonnits they turnit,
   The traiter Haddo o' thir heid,
An' slaid theire britheris an' their fatheris,
   An' spoilit an' left them for deid.

11. Than Murry cried to tak thi auld Gordone,
An' mony ane ran wi' speid;
But Stuart o' Inchbraik had him stickit,
An' out gushit thi fat lurdane's bleid.

12. Than they teuke his twa sones *quick* an' hale,
An' bare them awa' to Aberdene;
But sair did our guide quine lament
The waefu' chance that they were tane.

13. Erle Murry lost mony a gallant stout man;
Thi hopefu' laird o' Thorniture,
Pittera's sons, an' Egli's far fearit laird,
An' mair to mi unkend, fell doune.

14. Erle Huntly mist ten score o' his bra' men,
Sum o' heigh an' sum o' leigh degree,
Skeenis youngest son, thi pryde o' a' the clan,
Was ther fun' dead, he widna flee.

15. This bloody fecht wis fercely faucht
Octobris aught an' twinty day,
Crystis' fyſteen hunder thriscore yeir
An' twa will mark thi deidlie fray.

16. But now thi day maist waeſu' came,
That day the quine did grite her fill,
For Huntly's gallant stalwart son,
Wis heidit on thi heidin hill.

17. Fyve noble Gordones wi' him hangit were,
Upon thi samen fatal playne;
Crule Murry gar't thi waefu' quine luke out,
And see hir lover an' liges slayne.

18. I wis our quine had better frinds,
I wis our countrie better peice;
I wis our lords wid na' discord,
I wis our weirs at hame may ceise.*

* From Ruddiman's "Weekly Magazine, or Edinburgh Amusement," July 30th, 1772, where it first appeared under the following note:—"We have been favoured with the following copy of an old Scots Ballad, by a gentleman of taste and

literature, which we do not remember ever to have seen in print; and, therefore, have given it a place for the sake of preservation. It is said to have been wrote by one FORBES, schoolmaster at Mary-culter, upon Dee-side."

It was reprinted in Ritson's "Scotish Songs," ii., p. 17; Aytoun's "Ballads of Scotland," i., p. 237; Maidment's "Scotish Ballads and Songs," i., p. 215; and "Ballad Minstrelsy of Scotland" (Glasgow, 1871), p. 503. It has been supposed that the "Forbes, Schoolmaster at Mary-culter" is an error for "William Forbes, Schoolmaster of Peterculter" (1725-32), author of "The Dominie Depos'd," but this is mere conjecture. The rough vigour of some of the lines would lead us to suppose that the present ballad had been furbished up from some traditionary version; but as it now stands it is one of the pseudo-antiques which found their way into print consequent on the interest aroused by the publication of Percy's Reliques.

V.—CULTER TO BANCHORY.

The sun shines bright upon bonnie Dee,
  And bright on its birken bowers,
And steals thro' the shade of the chestnut tree
  On the Baron's old grey towers.

BETWEEN Culter and Drum stations, the latter 10 miles from Aberdeen, the turnpike sweeps round the North side of Newmill Hill (328 feet). The parish of Drumoak is entered shortly after crossing the Burn of Culter, and has two railway stations, Drum and Park, the road again approaching the railway in the vicinity of the former. The estate of Drum (Mrs. Irvine, as curatrix of Alexander Forbes Irvine) occupies the greater part of the parish; a portion of the estate of Leys (Sir Thomas Burnett, Bart.) is within this parish; and also the estate of Park (James Penny).

Drum.

North-west of the station, and within sight of the railway, at the distance of about a mile, is Drum Castle, once a royal residence, and for centuries past the seat of one of the most ancient families in Aberdeenshire, whose romantic history would itself require a volume. Part of the building, a massive tower, is believed to have been erected by King William the Lion. The family dates its genealogy from a very distant period, the first Irvine of Drum coming from Dumfries-shire as armour-bearer to the Bruce. As a reward for faithful service the King made him a grant of the lands and forest of Drum, the charter, dated 4th October, 1324, being still extant. Previous to this grant, the forest formed part of the royal domains.

The Irvines of Drum have always taken a prominent part in national affairs, from the battle of Harlaw, in which Sir Alexander Irvine lost his life, to recent times. Cordial relations have also subsisted between the lairds of Drum and the citizens of Aberdeen, and the Sir Alexander Irvine of 1440 was appointed Captain and Governor of the city. Yet another Sir Alexander was created Earl of Aberdeen by Charles I., but the troubles during the civil war

Drum Castle.

prevented the patent passing the Great Seal. At that time the Drum family possessed extensive estates in different parts of the country, but confiscations and other misfortunes made a considerable change in their circumstances. The present proprietor is the twenty-second in succession. The modern part of the castle dates from 1619; adjoining it there is a small chapel of older date containing the family vault.

The ruins of the old church of Drumoak stand within the burial ground, close to the left bank of the Dee, Southward from Drum station. Beside them is St. Maik's Well, which preserves the name of the patron saint of the parish, which is locally known as Dalmaik. The church is mentioned in a Papal Bull, in 1157, under the name of "Dulmayok".

> He set me in a pleasance rare
> Of moor, and wood, and waters cool,
> As Lebanon divinely fair,
> As purple Tirzah, beautiful.

Park.

The present church of Drumoak is a neat Gothic building, erected in 1836, on the North side of the road, nearly half a mile from Park station. Between the station and the river is Keith's Muir, the traditional scene of an encounter between the Irvines of Drum and the Keiths. The Loch of Drum, known also as the Loch of Park, about a mile West from Park station, is a beautiful sheet of water fringed with trees. Drainage operations have reduced its area from 300 to 84 acres, and its average depth is now only about four feet. It is frequented by a large variety of water-fowl, including the water-hen, little grebe, heron, golden-eyed duck, widgeon, mallard, teal, and, in winter, geese, swans, and goosanders. There is no trout in the loch, but pike, perch, and eel are plentiful. At the North-east end is the "King's Well", so called, according to tradition, from having been used by the Kings of Scotland when hunting in the forest of Drum.

The railway and the road run close together all the way between Drum and Banchory, and the river is also near. The mansion house of Park is finely situated between the railway and the Dee, a little beyond the twelfth milestone. The name is derived from the lands having at one time formed part of the "Park" of Drum. It was indeed in the possession of the Irvine family for a period of nearly three hundred years prior to 1737. The mansion house was built in 1822, and is a handsome building in the Grecian style, with beautiful grounds. Near by stands a sculptured stone found in 1822 on Keith's Muir.

The Dee has changed its channel in many places; indeed, there is scarcely a mile below the Linn of Dee that does not bear evidence of that fact. A short distance to the South-west of Park House, opposite Castle Hill of Durris, the river has made a detour to the Eastward, enclosing a piece of ground now known as the Island of Dee.

THE LAIRD O' DRUM.

1. The Laird o Drum is a hunting gane,
All in a morning early,
And he did spy a well-far'd may,
Was shearing at her barley.

2. 'O will ye fancy me, fair may,
And let your shearing be, O,
And gang and be the lady o' Drum?
O will ye fancy me? O.'

3. 'I winna fancy you,' she says,
'Nor let my shearing be;
For I'm ower low to be Lady Drum,
And your miss I'd scorn to be.'

4. 'But ye'll cast aff that gown o grey,
Put on the silk and scarlet;
I'll make a vow, and keep it true,
You'll neither be miss nor harlot.'

5. 'Then dee you to my father dear,
   Keeps sheep on yonder hill;
To ony thing he bids me do
   I'm always at his will.'

6. He has gane to her father dear,
   Keeps sheep on yonder hill:
'I'm come to marry your ae daughter,
   If ye'll gie me your gude will.'

7. 'She'll shake your barn, and winna your corn
   And gang to mill and kill;
In time of need she'll saddle your steed;
   And I'll draw your boots mysell.'

8. 'O wha will bake my bridal bread,
   And wha will brew my ale,
And wha will welcome my lady hame,
   It's mair than I can tell.'

9. Four and twenty gentle knights
   Gied in at the yetts o Drum;
But nae a man lifted his hat
   Whan the lady o Drum came in.

10. But he has taen her by the hand,
   And led her but and ben;
Says, 'You'r welcome hame, my lady Drum,
   For this is your ain land.'

11. For he has taen her by the hand,
   And led her thro the ha;
Says, 'You'r welcome hame, my lady Drum,
   To your bowers ane and a'.'

12. Then he stript her o the robes o grey,
   Drest her in the robes o gold,
And taen her father frae the sheep-keeping,
   Made him a bailie bold.

13. Out it speaks his brother dear,
   Says, 'You've dune us great wrang;
You've married a wife below your degree,
   She's a mock to all our kin.'

14. Out then spake the Laird o Drum,
Says, 'I've dune you nae wrang;
I've married a wife to win my bread,
You've married ane to spend.

15. 'For the last time that I was married,
She was far abeen my degree;
She wadna gang to the bonny yetts o Drum
But the pearlin abeen her ee,
And I durstna gang in the room where she was
But my hat below my knee.'

16. When they had eaten and well drunken,
And all men bound for bed,
The Laird o Drum and his lady gay
In ae bed they were laid.

17. 'Gin ye had been o high renown,
As ye are o low degree,
We might hae baith gane down the streets
Amang gude companie.'

18. 'I tauld you ere we were wed
You were far abeen my degree;
But now I'm married, in your bed laid,
And just as gude as ye.

19. 'Gin ye were dead, and I were dead,
And baith in grave had lain,
Ere seven years were at an end,
They'd not ken your dust frae mine.' *

---

* Versions of this Ballad, more or less fragmentary, are found over great part of Scotland from Aberdeenshire to Haddingtonshire. Late tradition gives the lady's name as Margaret Coutts—but it has never been duly verified. Jervise in his "Epitaphs" notes that a Margaret Coutts was the second wife of Robert Irvine of Cults; she died in 1710, aged 45. Her husband died 1728, aged 89. The oldest copy that has come down to us is contained in a MS. Collection obtained in the north by James Skene of Rubislaw (1805-18), but dated by Scott, 1802-3. The earliest printed version is in "Kinloch's Ancient Scottish Ballads, 1827," and though said by him to be

Like silver shines the dimpling Dee,
That seeks with rapid speed the sea.

Crathes.

About 12 miles from Aberdeen the parish of Banchory-Ternan, in the county of Kincardine, is entered. Crathes station, in this parish, is 3 miles from Park, 14 from Aberdeen. Crathes is yearly increasing in popularity, as its scenery and situation deserve; it has now become a favourite resort of the citizens of Aberdeen in the summer and autumn months. The most interesting place in the neighbourhood is Crathes Castle, the fine grounds of which are occasionally open to the public.

The Castle is about a mile Westward from the station, in an excellent situation among fine woods overlooking the river, and possessing a simple variety of formal garden not uncommon in Scotland. It is the seat of Sir Thomas Burnett, Bart. of Leys, and is rather an imposing structure, dating from 1528, with modern additions. It is considered to be a good example of the Scoto-Franco style of architecture,

---

given from recitation, fourteen of the twenty-four stanzas he prints are from a manuscript in the handwriting of James Beattie, now among the Kinloch MSS. in Harvard University Library. Professor Child prints Beattie's text as his "A" version. We here give the ballad as printed in Child's "D" version, from Joseph Robertson's "Deeside Guide," on the whole, the best of all the texts we have, and undoubtedly locally gleaned. Stanza 8 is a commonplace in Scotish Balladry; and one verse, between stanzas 12 and 13—a palpable interpolation—has been omitted. In Robertson's own interleaved copy of his "Deeside Guide" is another MS. copy of the ballad, but the differences between it and the printed text are merely verbal and of no consequence. The air to which the ballad was sung may be found in Kinloch App. to p. 199, or in Christie's "Ballad Airs," Vol. i., p. 24.

somewhat similar to Glamis, Castle Fraser, and Craigievar, "consisting", as a technical authority says, "of the elements common to most of the northern mansions—a multitude of conical turrets, high crow-stepped gables, and angular dormer windows". In 1306 certain lands, once the property of the Wauchopes, were granted to the Burnetts, as well as the office of

Crathes Castle.

forester of Drum. The horn of office is still in the possession of the family; but in 1324 the appointment went, with the forest of Drum itself, to the Irvines. In 1324, Alexander de Burnard, an ancestor of the present proprietor, received from King Robert Bruce a grant of certain lands in Drumoak, together with lands in Skene and Banchory, "within his forest of Drom, and without the park of the said forest". The estate of Leys lies North and West from Crathes Castle, and till recent years contained a loch with a circumference of between two and three miles, known as the Loch of Leys, which in the march of agricultural science has completely disappeared by drainage. In the charter of 1324 it is styled the Loch of Banchory, with a ferry, an island, and fishings. At one time there was a fortified dwelling on the island, which was probably the residence of the Burnetts before the erection of Crathes Castle. It is worth recording that two ancient families living side by side on the banks of the Dee, each gave a Bishop to Salisbury—the famous Bishop Burnett having sprung from the family of Leys, and Bishop Douglass from that of Tilquhillie.

> Afore the fire fouk couldna sit for fear,
> For peats and clods cam' bungin' ben the flear.
> The parson cam' and sained the house wi' prayer,
> But still the clods were thuddin' here and there.

The farm of Baldarroch, to the North of Crathes station, acquired some notoriety in 1838-9 as the scene of certain mysterious manifestations attributed to witchcraft, which form the ground-work of Alexander Walker's humorous poem, *The Deil at Baldarroch*, in which he describes how

> The spoons an' dishes, knives an' forks,
> They frisk'd aboot as light as corks:
> An' cups an' ladles joined the dancin',
> An' thro' the house they a' gaed prancin'.

An official enquiry, which was deemed necessary, resulted in the discovery that two servant girls were the spiritualistic "mediums". The circumstances are also referred to in a pamphlet, *The Dance of Baldarroch* (? 1840), the concluding words of which are: "This is placed here to point out Baldarroch as the spot where superstition and witchcraft were last believed in Scotland, anno 1838". Another pamphlet, *Banchory-Ternan Sixty Years Ago*, by Rev. Charles Ogg, also devotes some space to the occurrence.

Two miles West from Crathes Castle, the Burgh of Banchory is entered.

THE BARON O LEYS.

1. The Baron o Leys to France is gane,
   The fashion and tongue to learn,
   But hadna been there a month or twa
   Till he gat a lady wi bairn.

2. But it fell ance upon a day
   The lady mournd fu sairlie;
   Says, Who's the man has me betrayed?
   It gars me wonder and fairlie.

3. Then to the fields to him she went,
   Saying, Tell me what they ca thee;
   Or else I'll mourn and rue the day,
   Crying, alas that ever I saw thee!

4. 'Some ca's me this, some ca's me that,
   Whatever name best befa's me;
   But when I walk thro Saint Johnstone's town
   George Burnett they ca' me.'

5. 'O wae's me, O wae's me, George Burnett,
   And alas that ever I saw thee!
   For I'm in love, sick, sick in love,
   And I kenna well fat to ca' thee.'

6. 'Some ca's me this, some ca's me that,
   Whatever name best befa's me;
   But when I am on bonnie Dee-side
   The Baron o Leys they ca me.'

7. 'O weal is me now, O Baron o Leys,
   This day that ever I saw thee!
 There's gentle blood within my sides,
   And now I ken fat they ca thee.

8. 'But ye'll pay down ten thousand crowns,
   Or marry me the morn;
 Else I'll cause you be headed or hangd
   For gieing me the scorn.'

9. 'My head is a thing I cannot well want,
   My lady loves me so dearly;
 But I'll deal the gold right liberally
   For lying ae night sae near thee.'

10. When word had gane to the Lady o Leys
   The baron had gotten a bairn,
 She clapped her hands, and this did say,
   'I wish he were in my arms!

11. 'O weal is me now, O Baron o Leys,
   For ye hae pleased me sairly;
 Frae our house is banishd the vile reproach
   That disturbed us late and early.'

12. When she looked ower her castle-wa,
   To view the woods sae rarely,
 There she spied the Baron o Leys
   Ride on his steed sae rarely.

13. Then forth she went her baron to meet,
   Says, Ye're welcome to me, fairly!
 Ye'se hae spice-cakes, and seed-cakes sweet,
   And claret to drink sae rarely. *

---

* This is the version in Buchan's "Ballads of the North of Scotland" (1828), which was reprinted in Robertson's "Deeside Guide" *verbatim*. We have, however, omitted the eight verses of idle repetition about "Clatter the Speens," and "Scour the Brass," which are now recognised as interpolations by a later hand. The earliest copy is in the Skene of Rubislaw MS. (1802-3); but Buchan's text is the one popularly known among the older natives of the district.

There is no foundation for the story of the ballad in the

VI.—BANCHORY.

In the old kirk-yard in Saint Ternan's howe,
The ash-trees spread in many a bough;
Oh, well may they spread, for their roots lie deep
Where the dead in their lairs lie fast asleep.

BANCHORY is the most popular place on the banks of the Dee. As a summer resort for Aberdonians and tourists it takes precedence, for numbers, over all others, while on holidays excursionists visit it literally in thousands. The railway station is 17 miles from Aberdeen, and is situated at the East end of the town. The parish of Banchory-Ternan (sometimes referred to as Upper Banchory) lies on both sides of the river, the larger part being on the North bank. The Hill of Fare protects Banchory from the cold winds of the North, and its Southern exposure also contributes to its advantages as a health and holiday resort. Unquestionably nature has done a great deal for Banchory; the marvel is that the century had begun before the nucleus of a town had been founded in such a delightful situation. But its builders have failed to make the best use of its natural advantages, and cannot be congratulated upon their success in laying it out.

The village was founded in 1805, but so early as

---

family history of the Burnetts of Leys; indeed "The Baron o Leys" along with the ballad of "Lord Aboyne" ("The Rantin Laddie") seem to be locally adapted versions of an earlier ballad, "The Linkin Laddie," fragments of which are in the Herd MSS., in the British Museum, and the hero of which, Scott says, was a brother of Boston, the celebrated author of "The Fourfold State" (*Laing's "Sharpe's Ballad Book,"* 1880). Music:—Johnson's "Museum," No. 237.

1324 there had existed, in the vicinity of the church, a cluster of houses known as the Kirktown, latterly Townhead, of which the railway made an end in 1853. The station now occupies the site, and the road, which formerly passed through Townhead, was diverted to the North. The church stood in the churchyard till 1824, when it was rebuilt on higher ground at the East end of the modern village. The church, with certain lands, was granted to the Abbot of Arbroath by King William the Lion. St. Ternan, the patron saint, died about 440, and is said to have been presented by Pope Gregory the Great with a bell called the "Ronnecht", which had a remarkable power—it followed St. Ternan, of its own accord, when he went on pilgrimage! It is suggested by Jervise that the small square bell found "a few years ago, when a pathway was being made along the brink of the river from Banchory Lodge to the railway station", was this famous "Ronnecht", but unfortunately it has disappeared. A still more precious relic associated with St. Ternan is also lost—a copy of the Gospel of St. Matthew, cased in silver and gold, which was preserved in Banchory till the Reformation. The "watch-house" in the churchyard has a bell bearing the inscription: PETRVS STENS ROTTERDAMI · ME · FECIT · A°· 1664 · SOLI · DEO · GLORIA.

For a considerable time previous to 1885 the village had a popularly elected "Town Council", but realising that its attractions, on sanitary grounds, might be considerably increased, it then adopted the Lindsay Act and became a police burgh. It has a Town Hall, at the West end of the village, and a regular water supply brought from the base of

Kerloch, five miles to the South. A handsome public park—the Burnett Park, presented by the late Sir Robert Burnett—at the West end of the Burgh, was opened in 1887. The Burgh also possesses a public hall, a monument to a distinguished scholar, Dr. Francis Adams of Banchory, who died in 1861, a granite fountain in memory of Lieut-Col. Burnett-Ramsay of Banchory Lodge, who died in 1865, and shews other evidences of advance with the times. Banchory Lodge is beautifully situated between the railway and the river, East of the road from the Burgh to the Dee, and was known (along with Arbeadie) as Cobleheugh previous to the erection of the bridge. Raemoir House is a modern building about two miles North from the village; near it are the ruins of the castle of Cluny-Crichton, erected in 1666 by George Crichton of Cluny. The estate of Raemoir formerly belonged to the great family of Skene.

The Dee is crossed by an iron truss bridge of 175 feet span, having also three small stone arches, built in 1798 and repaired in 1829, after suffering damage from the flood of that year. At the South end of the bridge is the entrance gate to Blackhall Castle, where the South Deeside road may be said to end for a time, as there is no public road along the South bank of the river till the neighbourhood of Bridge of Potarch is reached. What might be called the South road proceeds up the Feugh by the village of Strachan to Whitestone (Feughside Inn), and thence goes North-westward through Birse to Potarch.

Here clear Dee hastens down,
By park and castled steep,
To gain the stern grey town,
And wind-vexed deep.

The artistic façade of the previous entrance gate to Blackhall Castle was surmounted by the figure of a goat—the crest of the proprietor—with the motto "Che sara sara", "What will be will be". Cut life-size, it was a striking piece of sculpture, never failing to attract attention, the motto also being frequent matter of conjecture. The approach to the castle is about two miles in length, and it is difficult to imagine one more picturesque. The river flows closely alongside the avenue ; on the South side there is high wooded ground sloping from Scolty. The present building, erected by the proprietor, Mr. James T. Hay, is a beautiful structure on a splendid site with a secluded position. It is very noticeable, however, from both the railway and the North road, the grey granite of the castle being conspicuous among the woods by which it is surrounded. The Russells had a small burial ground, "The Howff", a few yards Westward from the castle. It is now simply an enclosure of four plain walls, for the entrance door has been built up, and the slab with their arms has fallen to the ground, as though in response to the motto.

The finely wooded Hill of Scolty (982 feet) lies in the parish of Strachan, about a mile and a half to the South-west of the Bridge of Dee. It is surmounted by a tower erected to the memory of the late General Burnett of Banchory Lodge, who died in 1839, both hill and tower being visible from considerable distances. The trees on the summit of the hill now conceal the prospect formerly enjoyed here, and the tower has become unavailable as vantage-ground. A mile further West is the Hill of Goauch (1104 feet).

On the opposite (East) side of the Feugh is the old Castle of Tilquhillie, which, dating from the 16th century, has degenerated to a farmhouse.

> Tilquhillie stands on the old, old lands,
> And the name of the Douglas is there.

About 1479 the estate of Tilquhillie, which formed part of the Kirk-lands of Banchory, passed into the possession of David Douglas, a cadet of Douglas of Dalkeith, in which family, with the exception of a short break, it has since remained, the present proprietor being the fourteenth in lineal descent. The laird of 1562 took part in the battle of Corrichie under the Earl of Huntly. He was ultimately pardoned, but had to live for some time in retirement at Tilquhillie under the name of "James the Grieve"; he built the present castle in 1576, "a plain, but massive specimen of a Scottish house of the end of the sixteenth century". About 1647 it was garrisoned by the Covenanters, the then laird being an officer in the Royal Army. The castle commands an extensive Eastward prospect, and, with its ivy-clad walls, its crow-stepped gables, and its moss-covered roof, is suggestive of the romantic past. The original iron door is still in use.

The principal estates and land-owners in Banchory-Ternan are: Arbeadie, Captain Thomas B. Ramsay; Blackhall, James T. Hay; Durris, Henry R. Baird; Glassel, Captain Charles Michell; Inchmarlo, Duncan Davidson; Knappach, James Collie; Leys, Sir Thomas Burnett, Bart.; Raemoir, Trustees of Mrs. Innes; and Tilquhillie, John W. E. J. Douglass.

Hark ! list how the sweet, mellow mavis is singin' ;
Chant on little birdie, I'll listen to thee,
Till the woods o' Tilquhillie wi' music are ringin '—
The hame o' my sires, by the clear, windin' Dee.

The Feugh. The scenery at Bridge of Feugh is among the finest on lower Deeside. The bridge itself is a rather plain structure, carrying the South road over the stream at a point about 350 yards above its confluence with the Dee, where—both above and below the bridge—the Feugh forms a picturesque "linn". Generally rivers have "falls" and "rapids" in the upper part of their course only, and, as they approach the end of their career, settle down to a tranquil ending ; but it is not so with the Feugh. Its banks are here lined with trees, and its channel is rocky and uneven in the extreme. The stream cannot be said to flow ; it rather writhes and dashes over and between rocks, and, viewed on the occurrence of a "spate", is an impressive and magnificent sight. The Feugh is a noted salmon and trout stream, as many as fifty salmon having been caught in one day in the large pool below the bridge. Crowds of visitors frequently watch salmon and trout leaping the cascades in the summer and autumn. The Feugh joins the Dee at right angles, but evidently it had originally an Easterly-inclined course to its confluence. It is said that the artificial change of channel was indirectly the cause of the formation of the islands below. Finger-posts at the bridge give the following distances : Kirkton of Durris, 4¾ miles ; Mill Inn, Maryculter, 10½ miles ; Aberdeen, 18 miles ; Kirkton of Strachan, 3 miles ;

Whitestone (Feughside Inn), 5¼ miles; Bridge of Bogindreep (Dye), 4¼ miles; Bridge of Dye, 8 miles.

The Feugh rises in the parish of Birse, on the borders of Forfarshire, on the Northern slope of Mudlee Bracks (2259 feet) and Hill of Cammie (2028 feet), and has a course of about 20 miles. Flowing through the Forest of Birse, it passes on the left the fragmentary ruin of an old castle, which in style had closely resembled Knock.

> High on the bonny hills o' Birse
> Stan's good Sir Thomas' tower,
> An' far an' wide the oak tree spreads
> That shades his lady's bower.

It is said to have been built by Sir Thomas Gordon of Cluny about the middle of the 16th century. In the beginning of the 18th century certain Highland Caterans took possession, for a time, of the then deserted building; one is tempted to associate the verses on page 89 with the temporary residence of the rievers in Birse Castle.

The mansion house of Finzean is about a mile North from the Feugh, three miles from Whitestone. It is a fine building, part of it dating from 1686, nearly hidden from view by a gigantic hedge of holly, and is pleasantly situated in a richly wooded district. The Farquharsons of Finzean are sprung from Donald, the eldest son of Findla Mohr, laird of Castletown of Braemar, and the laird of Finzean, owing to the failures of the male line on the other side of the water, now claims to be chief of the Farquharson clan. About half a mile above Whitestone the Feugh is joined by a considerable tributary, the Water of Aven. Whitestone was formerly a great halting

Bridge of Feugh.

place for drovers on the Cairn O' Mount road from Fettercairn to Potarch. Here a road leaves the Feugh and holds North-westward to Potarch by a steep slope, reaching its highest point at Corsedarder, a stone marking the spot where, according to tradition, Dardanas, a Pictish king, was slain, an immense cairn in an adjoining wood covering his grave.

Easter Clune, another ancient hunting seat of the Bishops of Aberdeen, stood on the South side of the Feugh about two miles West from Whitestone. A very small portion of the walls of the old building still remains. A little to the East of it there is an old burial ground ; on the West was the church.

> Oh, bonny are our greensward howes,
> Where through the birks the burnie rows,
> And the bee bums and the ox lows,
> And saft winds rustle,
> And shepherd lads on sunny knowes
> Blaw the blythe fustle.

Strachan.

The village of Strachan lies on the left bank of the Feugh, about 3½ miles South-west from Banchory. The church of Strachan formerly belonged to the Cathedral of Brechin, and in 1574 was served along with those of Nigg and Maryculter. There is mention of the family of Strachan of Strachan as early as 1100. The old church stood within the burial-ground, but a new one was erected in 1866 on the North side of the road. In front of it is a fountain, dated 1866, "in remembrance of William Burnett Ramsay of Banchory Lodge". About half a mile West from the village the Water of Dye joins the Feugh on the right bank. Another half mile Westward is Castle Hill, where Alan the Durward is said to have had a residence, and where, in 1351, Fraser, Thane of Cowie, had a stronghold. A farm called Bowbutts, at the East end of the village, and several circular mounds in the neighbourhood recall the times when the local bow-men practised archery.

The Water of Aven (which gives name to the parish) rises on the water-shed of three counties—Aberdeen, Kincardine, and Forfar. Its source is a very small tarn, named Loch Tennet, about a mile North-west of Mount Battock (2555 feet). The Aven, from source to mouth, separates Kincardineshire on the right bank from Aberdeenshire on the left bank. It has a course of eight miles, and is a fair trouting stream. Peter Hill (2023 feet) stands on the left bank.

The Water of Dye rises on the Eastern slope of Mount Battock, and has a course of about fifteen miles. Its principal tributary on the right bank, from the South, is the Water of Charr, Eastward of which is Cairn O' Mount (1488 feet), on the boundary between the parishes of Strachan and Fordoun. About two and a half miles North of Cairn O' Mount the Dye is joined by Spital Burn. As the name implies, a "Spital" or Hospital had existed here in old times for the accommodation of travellers. A public-house naturally succeeded the Spital, but it, too, disappeared when the drover took to the railway. That the public-house had, at times, an indifferent reputation, may be inferred from an intimation made in Strachan church: "The Cairn O' Mount road is quite safe now; there's honest folk at the Spital". Indeed, at one time the road was infested with robbers, and human life was not always safe. The name "Thieves' Bush" is still retained by a ravine a few hundred yards North from the Cairn. A mile below Spital Burn is Bridge of Dye, a very old structure, built by Sir Alexander Fraser of Durris, assisted by "mortifications". By Scottish Acts of Parliament of 1681 and 1685, tolls were authorised for keeping the bridge in repair. To the West of the bridge is Glendye Lodge, a beautifully situated shooting-box. Part of the glen has recently been fenced for deer.

> Mount Battock, how dark is the cloud on thy brow,
> How grateful its gloom to the valley below!
> For the hand of the riever has smitten so sore,
> The days of our mourning will never be o'er.
> He came in the night; he has taken and slain
> The wale of our flocks and the flower of our men;
> The fold now is silent, the shieling is still,
> No herd in the valley, no flock on the hill.

Between the Waters of Aven and Dye there is a hilly range culminating, at the upper end, in Mount Battock, between which and Clochnaben, a distance of about four miles, the ground is much broken up by "moss hags", so much so that the walk between these two points of the range is sometimes the reverse of agreeable. About a mile North-eastward from Clochnaben is Mount Shade (1662 feet), the deep narrow gorge—visible from considerable distances—between the two hills being known as the Devil's Bite or the Slacks of Dye (1300 feet).

> Clochnaben an' Bennachie
> Are twa lan' marks o' the sea.

Clochnaben (1900 feet) is, with the possible exception of Mount Battock, the most noticeable summit between the Aven and the Dye. Remarkable for its great outstanding mass of granite, like a gigantic wart, and of the same formation as the rocky peaks of Ben Avon, it is readily recognisable and clearly visible from many distant points. From Aberdeen to Clochnaben is a favourite "day excursion", the view well rewarding the little exertion required. From Banchory to Bridge of Dye is a distance of about 9 miles, and the walk from the bridge to the "Cloch" (stone—the whole name signifying "stone of the mountain") is about three miles further. The ascent, however, is generally made from Feughside Inn; the return journey may be varied by Glendye Lodge and the Cairn O' Mount road. The projecting rock, to which the mountain owes its name, is 95 feet in height, and has been produced by the wearing away of the softer material in its immediate vicinity; but this natural explanation was not accepted by the natives, as may be seen from verses written by Rev. George Knowles, minister of Birse, who died in 1789. According to the poem, the stone formerly lay "low in a plain", but used in a contest between "The D-v-l and his Dame", the last stanza thus accounts for its present position:

"Have at you now, you Beldame", roared the fiend,
And hurl'd the rock through the resounding skies;
Dreadful it fell, and crush'd his breathless friend,
And there entombed Her Hellish Highness lies!

(Mount Battock and Clochnaben are fully described in Vol. 1 of *The Cairngorm Club Journal*).

The following are the estates and proprietors in the parish of Strachan: Strachan, Captain Thomas B. Ramsay; Blackhall, James T. Hay; Invery, John W. E. Douglass; and Lands of Strachan, Sir John R. Gladstone, Bart.

VII.—BANCHORY TO ABOYNE.

Good news, good news, my lady gay,
The Lord o' Aboyne is comin';
He's scarcely twa miles frae the place,
Ye'll hear his bridles ringin'.

I.—By Rail.

THE railway diverges Northward from the river as Banchory station is left, and, nearing it again at Dess, runs alongside it from Aboyne to Ballater. Lumphanan station is the apex of this detour. Wood and moorland are the chief features of the landscape till Glassel is reached, after which the prospect brightens, tree-clad heights at intervals giving a pleasing variety to the scenery.

Glassel.

The first station beyond Banchory is Glassel, distant 4½ miles. It lies within the parish of Kincardine O'Neil, close to its Banchory border. Glassel House is a little to the right of the station, on the burn of Canny. Campfield House, also in the parish of Kincardine O'Neil, has a beautiful site on the South-western slope of the Hill of Fare.

Torphins.

Torphins, 2½ miles beyond Glassel, is the usual station for the village of Kincardine O'Neil, from which it is 3 miles distant. A village has sprung up in the neighbourhood of the station, and is yearly increasing in importance. Alexander Ross, author of "Helenore", was born at Inchley near the station; John Anderson, the "Wizard of the North", was also born in the neighbourhood. Beltie Burn, as Burn of Canny is called in its upper reaches, here flows on the South side of the railway. Learney House, about 2 miles North, is a large, plain, substantial building. Craigmyle House, within a mile to the Eastward, is an ancient mansion, built by Alexander Farquharson of Monaltrie, slightly modernised, standing among some fine old trees. The ruins of Castle Maud stand at the West end of Moss Maud, about a quarter of a mile on the East side of the road leading from Torphins to Kincardine O'Neil. Nothing authentic is known of its history. "Tradition says it was formerly a hunting seat of one of the Bishops of Aberdeen, and that it existed in the days of Bruce, his Queen spending a night there. However, the date of its erection is unknown, and, whatever might have been inviting about the spot at that time, there are now no peculiar attractions". The ruins are by no means imposing, the walls being only about six feet in height; the inside dimensions are about twenty feet by seventeen, so that the building had probably been of the nature of a tower or keep. There are indications of outworks on tbe east side.

> O'er the Mounth they chased him then
> Intil the woods of Lumphanan,
> . . . .
> This Macbeth slew they there,
> Intil the woods of Lumphanan.

Lumphanan.

Lumphanan station is 3 miles from Torphins, and 27 from Aberdeen. The turnpike from Aberdeen, *via* Garlogie and Raemoir, runs along the South side of the line all the way from Torphins to

Lumphanan. Between these stations the deep hollow of the Beltie Burn, popularly called "Satan's Den", is crossed by a viaduct. The village of Lumphanan owes its existence to the railway.

Findrack House is situated on the Beltie Burn, about a mile above the viaduct, on the West side of Learney Hill (1150 feet); the estate has been in the possession of the Fraser family since 1670. Pitmurchie House lies on the South side of the railway, about three quarters of a mile South from the viaduct; the estate once formed part of Findrack. Beltie Burn is here the boundary between the parishes of Kincardine O'Neil and Lumphanan.

The parish of Lumphanan, the death scene of Macbeth on 15th August, 1057, when he engaged the forces of Malcolm III. in battle, is, from an antiquarian and historical point of view, one of the most interesting on Deeside. Macbeth's Cairn and the Peel Bog are themselves quite sufficient to make the district notable.

The church is about half a mile South-west from the station, on the South side of the railway. Close to it is a well known as Macbeth's Well; while about a quarter of a mile further South is the farm of Cairnbathie with "Macbeth's Stone", marking the spot where, according to tradition, Macbeth was wounded. Cairnbathie is said to be a corruption of Cairnbeth. Macbeth's Cairn, however, is about a mile to the North of Cairnbathie, on Perkhill, and is believed to mark the site of the King's grave. The Cairn is now a great flat mass of stones, with a well-like opening in the centre, and is enclosed by a dyke and surrounded by young trees. There are other cairns on Perkhill, which render it very probable that it was the scene of some great conflict—a supposition borne out by "finds" in the neighbourhood.

The Peel Bog lies a quarter of a mile to the South-west of the church, close to the North-west side of the railway. It is a circular earthen mound, about 12 feet in height and 46 yards in diameter, surrounded by a moat. Its existence probably dates from the 12th or 13th century. The Burn of Lumphanan evidently supplied the water for the moat. The flood of 1829 laid bare the sluice through which the water left the moat. A wooden fort was probably erected on the mound, and occupied at one time by the Durwards. On 21st July, 1296, Edward I. received here the submission of Sir John de Malvill. About the year 1400, possibly, the wooden building was replaced by one of stone, which latterly gave way to a more modern structure. Previous to 1782 the remains of a building were visible on the top of the mound. It was known as Haa-ton House—a corruption most probably of Halton, the name of an adjoining estate. A zealous agriculturist was responsible for the removal, for building purposes, of the crumbling ruins.

The remains of the Castle of Auchinhove are about one and a quarter miles South-west from the Peel Bog. There is little to indicate its former existence, but the old ash trees and the causewayed approach tell of a nobler building than the present ruined farm steading. Auchinhove belonged to the Duguids from about the year 1434. The representative of the family joined the Pretender in the '45 rebellion, and had his house burned by a party of the Duke of Cumberland's soldiers. The Houff, about half a mile

North-west from the Castle, had, in remote times, been a place of some strength, as is still evident from traces of ancient buildings. It ultimately became the burial place of the Duguids, a descendant of which family recently acquired the estate. *The Statistical Account* (1793) says, "Very lately above £100 sterling, all in Queen Anne's shillings, were found by two herds . . . near Auchhove . . . Tradition says that it is only a part of 50,000 merks hid here in 1745 by one Malcolm, a servant belonging to Mr. Duguid of Auchhove, who unfortunately joined in the rebellion, and that the rest was secreted in a man's boot".

About three quarters of a mile Eastward from Cairnbathie, on Stot Hill (923 feet), is Cairn Mude, said to have been built in memory of a Colonel Mude, who was killed in a duel fought near by.

Glenmillan House is about three quarters of a mile North-east from the station. The estate was formerly called Cloak.

The Tarland road (Aberdeen to Tarland *via* Echt) passes through the parish on the North side of Perkhill.

Proceeding from Lumphanan station towards Aboyne, the farm of Auchlossan will be passed about mid-way between Peel Bog and Dess station, the steading being on the East side of the railway. The farm was largely formed by draining the Loch of Auchlossan, which, according to *The Statistical Account*, was nearly a mile long, and more than half as broad at the South end. Pike and eel were plentiful—the former attaining a weight of 25 lbs.—while sea-gulls, ducks, geese, and swans frequented the loch, and the neighbourhood was considered one of the best snipe shooting spots in Scotland. The existence of the loch was not, however, advantageous to health, and it was resolved to reclaim it. The reclamation, commenced in 1860, was successfully carried out by Mr. J. W. Barclay, and was one of the most extensive agricultural operations of the kind ever attempted in Scotland.

The estates and proprietors in the parish of Lumphanan are: Finzean, Dr. Robert Farquharson, M.P.; Pitmurchie, James H. Bower; Glenmillan, Trustees of the late Robert Smith; Camphill, Alexander F. Wight; Camphill and Kintocher, Trustees of Lord Sempill; Findrack (part of), Mrs. Fraser; Findrack (part of), William N. Fraser; and Auchinhove, Charles S. Leslie Duguid.

Dess.

Dess is a small station (the nearest to the village of Kincardine O'Neil) 2½ miles from Lumphanan. Near the railway a flat circular stone, with a hole in it, may be observed; it formed part of a Whin Mill. Passing the old church and the picturesque Loch of Aboyne on the right, Aboyne station is reached, 3 miles from Dess and 32½ from Aberdeen.

II.—By Road.

The blackbird whistled loud and clear,
The mavis lilted back for glee,
And linties trilled their slender strains
Among the whins by winding Dee.

As already indicated there is no direct South road between Banchory and Aboyne. The Feugh reached, the "South" road is continued to Whitestone, where, entering the parish of Birse, it passes by the little village of Marywell, and thence to the church of

Birse, where it again approaches the Dee, near which it generally runs the whole way to Balmoral.

The North road, which keeps pretty close to the river and passes through the village of Kincardine O'Neil, forms a very pleasant walk or drive. The railway left behind, the view is, if rather restricted, very prettily bounded on the South by tree-clad Scolty. About two miles West from Banchory, the mansion house of Inchmarlo, pleasantly situated on the North side of the road, will be passed on the right; on the left, on the other side of the Dee, will be observed the stately building of Blackhall Castle. The Burn of Canny joins the Dee at Invercanny, a small hamlet, a short distance East of the 20th mile stone.

Aberdeen Water-works.

A few hundred yards above Invercanny the huge pipe of the Aberdeen Water-works crosses the Canny, the first reservoir, with two filter beds, being a short distance to the West. Frequent indications of the Water-works, in the shape of iron ventilating pillars, will have been observed all the way up. The "intake", where the water is drawn from the Dee, is still further Westward, at Cairnton, on the South side of the hill of that name, at a suitably retired spot, where the river flows over rock between well-wooded banks. There is little to see at the "intake"; yet there, 23 miles from Aberdeen, about 6,000,000 gallons of water are daily diverted from the Dee at a point 224 feet above sea level. A few yards below the "intake" there is a neat little building covering a sluice to cut off the water when its condition, or other circumstance, renders that course necessary. This building has an inscription giving the date of the commencement of the works (21st April, 1864), the date of opening (16th October, 1866), &c. The water is first conveyed, partly through a tunnel, 760 yards long, cut in gneiss rock, to a reservoir at Invercanny, about a mile East of Cairnton. Here there is storage for 10,000,000 gallons, as well as two filter beds. The opening ceremony was performed by the Queen at Invercanny. The total cost of the works has been over £160,000.

Westward of the Canny the Hills of Cairnton (427 feet) and Trustach (587 feet), two pleasantly wooded eminences, lie between the road and the river. The forest of Trustach was situated near the confluence of the Canny with the Dee; it was granted in the beginning of the 13th century by Alan the Durward to the Abbey of Arbroath, and latterly was made a "free forest". On the East side of the Hill of Trustach traces of old earthworks may be observed, which have been conjectured to belong to a Roman camp. The summit of the Hill of Trustach is about a quarter of a mile South-east of the 22nd mile-stone, shortly after passing which Horn Burn is crossed. The river is now close on the left; on the right is Sluie Hill with Sluie Woods, and at the 24th mile-stone Bridge of Potarch is reached.

A deep
And solemn harmony pervades
The hollow vale from steep to steep,
And penetrates the glades.

Potarch.

At Potarch the great North road over Cairn O' Mount by one of the "chief passages from the Tay to the Dee", formerly crossed the river by a ford at

Inchbaire, a little below the bridge. It was at this ford that Edward I. crossed the Dee on his way to and from Kildrummy Castle. The ford was liable to frequent interruptions from floods and ice, and the want of a bridge was much felt, owing to the great traffic that formerly passed along there. According to *The New Statistical Account* a collection was made sometime between 1698 and 1706, in the church of Boindie, to assist in "building an bridge over Dee at Pittarch". It was not, however, till the beginning of the present century that the bridge, which is quite a picturesque structure, came into actual existence. The length is 200 feet, and there are three arches, the largest of which has 70 feet span. On 19th October, 1812, when the bridge was nearly completed, loose trees, which were being floated down the river, broke the structure, almost entirely demolishing it; but it was rebuilt the following year. The flood of 1829 considerably damaged the piers, part of the rock (coarse red porphyry full of flaws) on which the foundations were built being completely torn away by the impetuous stream. There is an Inn (recently enlarged) at the South end, erected at the same time as the bridge, the markets formerly held at Marywell being then removed to Potarch. A finger-post here gives the following distances: Ballogie, 3 miles; Balfour, 3¾ miles; Aboyne, 6¼ miles; Whitestone, 4 miles; Marywell, 2½ miles.

About sixty yards above the bridge the river runs in a rocky channel, the narrowest part, about 15 feet broad, being called "Young's Leap". Here a tinker, John Young, having killed a brother "gipsy chief", leaped across the Dee to escape apprehension. He was afterwards captured, and executed in Aberdeen in 1801.

Shortly after passing the 25th mile-stone, the road is joined on the right by the turnpike from Aberdeen *via* Garlogie, Raemoir, and Torphins. A direction-post at the fork gives the following distances: (by Deeside) Potarch, ¼ mile; Banchory, 8 miles; Aberdeen, 25¼ miles—(by Torphins) Aberdeen, 23½ miles. A few yards further along, on the right, will be observed Borrowstone House. There was formerly a small hamlet at Borrowstone, with the principal Inn of the district, where for many years Justice of Peace Courts and Presbytery Meetings were held. About half a mile North was Kincardine Lodge, a mansion-house built towards the end of last century by John Grant; but from the fact of his having formerly been a tailor, the natives dubbed the building "Needle Ha'". The present structure, one of the largest mansions on Deeside, was recently built, partly in the old Scottish Baronial style, by Mrs. Pickering, and is known as Kincardine. A short distance beyond Borrowstone House the village of Kincardine O'Neil is reached, 26 miles from Aberdeen.

Ride fast, spair neither horse nor gear;
Through darksome pass and lainlie glen
Till fair Kincardine's haughs appear.

Kincardine O'Neil.

The situation of the village of Kincardine O'Neil is very agreeable, the scenery in the neighbourhood being exceedingly pleasant, and enhanced by the retired nature of the locality. The nearest railway stations are Dess, about two miles to the West, and Torphins, about three miles to the North-east. Formerly it was a very busy place, as all the traffic along the North side of the Dee passed through it, and it was also a halting place for drovers on their Southward journeys. At one time it was the only post-office for upper Deeside, there being none to the Westward.

The East end of the village was formerly called "Cochran's Croft", and even yet some speak of the "two villages of Kincardine O'Neil and Cochran". According to tradition, Cochran's Croft was a royal grant to the tenant in return for kindly entertainment.

> Of all the hostelries so fair,
> Built for the traveller's dwelling,
> On Deeside far beyond compare
> Kincardine is excelling.

This on the authority of Joseph Robertson, travestying the lines of a great poet. In his time the Inn at Kincardine O'Neil was a great favourite with travellers. In 1233, Alan the Durward erected at Kincardine O'Neil an hospital, which, it would appear, stood between the village and the present ferry over the Dee, where of old there was probably a bridge. St. Erchard is stated to have been the patron of the church about 933. The present church, built in 1861, is on the North side of the road. The ivy-covered ruins of the former building, which was burned about the year 1740, stand opposite, the area within the old walls being used as burial ground for the heritors of the parish. In the latter part of the last century, the markets (as in certain other Scottish parishes) encroached upon the churchyard; so much so, indeed, that goods were exposed for sale on the tombstones. "Many hundreds of persons assemble themselves in the kirkyard with horses, creels, and baggage of all kinds; some let their horses, several scores in number, run loose among the graves, and others tie them up by the sides of the church as to stalls; some . . . erect tents and booths, while others expose their wares upon the graves of the dead, and in the very porch of the church", and greater indecencies followed at night. On market days, in May and September, provisions (liquid and solid) were sold in almost every house in the village so recently as 1834; the markets were held on Barthol Muir, about a quarter of a mile above the village.

A small eminence, Gallow Hill, overlooks the village on the North. The Neil Burn, from which the parish derives part of its name, flows by the West side of Gallow Hill and through the village. A little to the East of the burn, above the church, is St. Erchard's Well. At the West end of the village is a neat Episcopal church with a burial-ground.

Edward I., with his retinue, spent a night in the village while on his Southward march in 1296. An old rhymster tells us that

> O' followers he haed a flock,
> Left neither capon, hen, nor cock,
> Na, nor butter, bread, nor cheese,
> Else my informant tells me lees,
> An' warst o' a' I'm wae to tell,
> They left them neither maut nor ale.

The Queen made a brief halt here on her first journey up Deeside in 1848.

Dess House is conspicuously situated on rising ground on the North side of the road, near the 27th mile-stone. Carlogie, on the opposite side of the river, has also an excellent, though rather low, position. The Dess Burn enters the Dee a short distance Westward, and drives several mills, wool, saw, and meal, in the vicinity of the bridge which crosses it. A direction-post at the bridge gives the following distances: Kincardine O'Neil, 1½ miles; Banchory, 9½ miles; Aberdeen, 27½ miles; Dess Station, ⅓ mile; Lumphanan, 3 miles; Alford 15¼ miles. A few yards to the West of the bridge a large flat circular stone, with a hole in the centre, is built into the dyke on the South side of the road. It is supposed to have been used for the erection of a gibbet.

A little North from the bridge, on the road leading to Dess station, the Sloc (or Slog) o' Dess, a picturesque little waterfall, 15 feet high, will be seen on the right. Passing the Loch of Aboyne, the village of Charlestown of Aboyne, about 30½ miles from Aberdeen, is reached.

The estates and proprietors in the parish of Kincardine O'Neil are: Craigmyle, John Gordon; Learney, Lieut-Col. F. N. Innes; Kincardine and Stranduff, Mrs. Pickering; Dalhaikie, Duncan Davidson; Kebbaty, Lady Gordon Cathcart; Tornaveen and Findrack, William N. Fraser; Midbeltie, Trustees of the late James Allan; Campfield, George Collie; Easter Beltie, Trustees of the late William Adam and Trustees of the late Andrew Wilson; and Dess, Major Duncan Francis Davidson.

VIII.—ABOYNE.

The water-fowl glides on the breast of the lake,
The deer climbs the mountains, the fox threads the brake.

ABOYNE is deservedly one of the most popular places on Deeside. The village is neat and pleasant, built on an extensive flat, surrounded by magnificent highland scenery. It has many attractions for the tourist and the sportsman, and every accommodation for the "summer lodger".

The village is known as Charlestown, having been so named from Charles, first Earl of Aboyne. The Barony of Aboyne was on the left bank of the Dee, the old name of the burgh being Bunty. The tolbooth was demolished in the end of last century, "and all traces of the pot and gallows also are nearly effaced". There is an excellent village green where the markets are held, and golf, cricket, football, and other games are indulged in; there is also an annual gathering for Highland sports. A little to the South-east is a fever hospital for the accommodation of the neighbouring parishes.

Aboyne Castle, the residence of the Marquis of Huntly, "the Cock of the North", is about half a mile North from the village. From its associations it is the most important family seat on Deeside East of Balmoral; its history is practically the history of the district. It is stated to date as far back as the 11th century, and to have been a royal residence in the time of Alexander III. It was one of the Scottish castles handed over in 1291 to Edward, and was thereupon garrisoned by English troops. The estate of Aboyne was possessed in the 13th century by the Bissets, after whose disappearance it fell into the hands of the Knights Templars; and the castle was for

Aboyne Castle.

a time occupied by the Earl of Mar. In 1388, however, both castle and lands were in possession of the Gordons. "The present marquis is a descendant of the old chiefs of the Gordons through a younger son of the Marquis of Huntly, who was executed during the troubles of 1649. The title of Marquis of Huntly, though merged in that of Duke of Gordon till 1836, reverted, on the death of the last duke, to the descendants of the second son of the executed marquis, who had been created Earl of Aboyne in his own right. The title of Duke of Gordon has been re-created in the person of the present Duke of Richmond and Gordon, the heir female of the old Dukes of Gordon". The castle lies at a height of about 400 feet, encircled by extensive plantations, and almost surrounded by Tarland Burn, the old name of which was Allach. The trees are mostly oak, ash, elm, beech, birch, larch and spruce—a pleasant variety. A sculptured stone, 6½ feet high, removed from Loch Kinord, stands on a knoll near a small Druidical circle in the vicinity of the castle. It probably served as a market cross for an annual fair held near its former site. In the heat of the Reformation it was thrown into the loch, but many years afterwards it was recovered and set up on the shore. A Donside laird, seeing the neglected relic of antiquity, carried it off, but the Earl of Aboyne, on being informed of the removal, caused it to be erected upon its present site. Between the castle and Loch of Aboyne is an old oak known as the Skeulan tree, with a well of the same name. The "Pest" was believed to have been buried here, so in old times none would touch the branches. Skeulan is probably a corruption of St. Eunan, to whom the church of Aboyne was anciently dedicated. A few yards West from the tree is another well called the Lady's Well.

The Loch of Aboyne (437 feet) is a pretty sheet of water, made in 1834, having an area of about 32 acres, with several wooded islets, which add considerably to its beauty. The loch is frequently the scene of curling contests, and is about a mile North-east from the station, but there is a platform for use on special occasions.

The old church of Aboyne (formerly called Formaston) stood a few yards to the East of the loch, and a little to the West of the 29th mile-stone, where the name "Kirkton" tells of the time when the present village did not exist. The ruined house here was not the manse, as several writers (the present among them) have stated, but the mansion of a Farquharson, a cadet of the Invercauld family, whose small patrimony was swallowed up in the Aboyne estates. There are some interesting monuments in the old graveyard. What is known as "The Aboyne Ogham Stone" was found here—almost under the door-step of the old church—and removed for preservation to the castle. Within an enclosure lie the remains of the Inneses of Balnacraig and Ballogie. Balnacraig, now a farm-house, is on the South side of the Dee, about 4 miles East from Aboyne; there is another Balnacraig on the North side, formerly the property of the Chalmers family, but now part of the Finzean estates.

Nae langer could he stan' the sicht,
But back ran he wi' a' his micht,
For he was in a waefu' plicht
At the Red Cap o' Mortlich.

Ilk hair on's head stood like a rash,
Through dirt an' mire he on did splash,
To look ahint he widna fash,
For seein' the ghaist o' Mortlich.

He said the ghaist was claid wi' hair,
The beard it was three feet an mair.
The red cap blazed wi' sic a glare,
It dazzled's een on Mortlich.

An' just below the red cap rim,
He saw a visage dark and grim,
His heart grew wae, his een grew dim,
An' he wished he'd n'er seen Mortlich.

The hill of Mortlich (1248 feet), about a mile North from the Loch of Aboyne, is the highest point in the parish on the North side of the Dee, and is conspicuous from many places in the district. It is surmounted by a granite obelisk 60 feet high, with a cross, erected in 1868, inscribed: "Charles, 10th Marquis of Huntly. Died 18th Sept., 1863. Erected by Mary Antoinetta, his Widow, and the Tenantry of Aboyne". On the summit there are the remains of a pretty large enclosure, apparently an encampment, but perhaps used for securing cattle, &c., in troublous times. On its South-eastern slope is Little Hill (Knockbeg), where are the remains of a circular encampment with a "Pictish Road" leading down to Tilphoudie and the Muir of Dess. At Tilphoudie are the remains of a mansion-house which was at one time the residence of a branch of the Gordons, of whom Cochran of Balfour is a descendant; to the East is Hirnley, where the noted Peter Williamson was born. Thomas Innes of the Scots College, Paris, was born at Drumnagesk in 1662.

The Dee is crossed by a handsome suspension bridge at the South-west end of the village. In 1828 the Earl of Aboyne erected here a bridge which the flood of the following year swept away. He rebuilt it in 1831, the length between the points of suspension being 230 feet, and the height of the roadway above sea level 412 feet. It was reconstructed by the County Road Trustees in 1871. Near the South end of the bridge is a direction-post with the following distances: Marywell, 3¾ miles; Potarch, 5½ miles; Whitestone, 8¾ miles; Glentana House, 3¾ miles; Ballater, 11 miles; Balmoral, 19 miles. A little above the South end of the Bridge the Aulddinnie Burn enters the Dee. It forms the boundary between the Glen Tanner portion of Aboyne and the parish of Birse, the river being here the march between the two parishes. Before the erection of the suspension bridge over the Dee there was a ferry about 600 yards to the East; the ferryman during the '45 is said to be named in a well-known Jacobite song, of which the following is the first verse:

> Come boat me o'er, come row me o'er,
> Come boat me o'er to Charlie;
> I'll gie John Ross anither bawbee
> To ferry me o'er to Charlie.

"Owing to a great flood of the river Dee, John's boat, on which his name and residence were painted, was carried off, and safely landed on the coast of Norway; from which circumstance arose the saying, long used in the locality, 'Go to Norway like John Ross's boat'". Dinnie in his "Deeside Guide" identifies this ferryman with the boatman of the song, but there are good grounds for believing that Deeside has no connection with the verses.

The estates and proprietors in the parish of Aboyne are: Aboyne, Trustees of the Marquis of Huntly; Glentana and part of Aboyne (Castle, &c.),

Sir William Cunliffe Brooks, Bart.; Drumnagesk, Marriage Contract Trustees of Admiral Sir Arthur and Lady Farquhar; Dess, Major Duncan Francis Davidson; Cromar, J. C. Barclay Harvey; Balnacraig, William E. Nicol; and Finzean, Dr. Robert Farquharson, M.P.

> There, tow'ring Keen o'erlooks the tenfold cloud,
> And shoots its conic head into the sky,
> Whilst sable mists its sloping sides enshroud,
> And half way hide it from the wond'ring eye.

Glentanner.

Glentanner, as a parish, is now united with Aboyne. The upper part of the glen, however, is in the united parish of Glenmuick-Tullich-Glengairn. At a remote period Glentanner and Inchmarnoch (now also in Glenmuick-Tullich-Glengairn) formed a parish.

The Water of Tanner is a considerable tributary of the Dee. It rises on Hare Cairn, at an altitude of about 2250 feet, about two miles West from Mount Keen, on the Forfarshire boundary; and, after flowing about 12 miles in a North-easterly direction, joins the Dee about a mile South-west from Aboyne. Its chief tributary is the Water of Allachy, which receives the Water of Gairney little more than half a mile above its confluence with the Tanner. The Gairney and the Allachy rise on the Forfarshire march to the East of Mount Keen (3077 feet), and drain the Northern sides of Braid Cairn (2907 feet), Cock Cairn (2387 feet), and Hill of Cat (2435 feet). The glen belonged to Sir William C. Brooks, Bart. (recently deceased), by whom it was converted into a deer forest. Sir William, since he came to Deeside over thirty years ago, spent a vast amount of money in the glen, and has beautified it in numberless ways. Morven, it may be noted, bulking prominently to the North-westward, is seen to advantage as the glen is approached.

The South road crosses the Tanner at Bridge of Ess, about half a mile above its confluence with the Dee. From Bridge of Ess to Bridge of Aboyne the distance is 1¾ miles, to Bridge of Dinnet 3¼ miles, and to Bridge of Ballater 9¾ miles. Here the bed of the Tanner is rocky, the banks are lined with trees, and to the natural picturesqueness of the scene is added an ivy-clad square tower which guards the bridge. On the left is Red Craig of Craigendinnie, appropriately named, covered with heather, with a few trees dotting the summit. Walking on, the Bridge of Tanner, narrow and high-centred, is reached. Here the mansion house comes into view, and the tourist, looking upon it for the first time, may well halt and enjoy the prospect. The glen is not wide, and the hills forming it at this point are of no great altitude, but the whole scene is beautiful. There is now little cultivated land, but several neat cottages have been built in the glen. The Bridge of Tanner was erected by General Wade to be used instead of the ford a little higher up the stream in connection with Fir Mounth road, along which marched the armies of Edward I. in 1296 and 1303, and Montrose in 1645. There is now, at the well by the road-side, where these hostile armies passed, an inscription giving the Highland welcome, *Cead Mille Failte*.

The mansion house was built by the late Sir William C. Brooks, and, while an unobtrusive building, is elegantly artistic and of considerable dimensions, rendering it one of the most important in the valley of the Dee. The offices, kennels, and other buildings in connection are built and finished in a manner shewing the individuality of, and reflecting much credit on their late owner. The lakes, above the mansion house, constructed for salmon culture, also add to the beauties of the scene. On the opposite (right) bank of the Tanner is the Episcopal Church of St. Lesmo, built by the late Sir William C. Brooks upon the ruins of the mansion house of Braeline. This old mansion had itself been built with the material of a ruined fortification—of which nothing authentic is known—of some local importance, as evinced by the ornamental archway, with stanchion holes, yet extant, and re-inserted in the church. The church is heather-thatched, with an open timber roof formed by natural wood; above the unplaned couplings hang antlers of deer, whose skins are used for pew coverings. The windows are filled with appropriately coloured glass. St. Lesmo, who died in 731, is credited with the introduction of Christianity in this neighbourhood. There is a burial-ground in connection with the church; near which is St. Lesmo's Well, inscribed, "Drink, weary Pilgrim, Drink and Pray". Appropriately enough, the "Sanctuary" of the forest surrounds the church. Formerly the haugh here was but a barren outspread of the Tanner; now, by means of sewage cultivation, excellent grass is produced, and at least four times as many cattle are fed as in former times The scenery in this neighbourhood is very grand. The wooded glen forms a noble picture, with the mansion house near by, and the obelisk-topped Mortlich in the distance.

Above the junction of the Allachy with the Tanner is the East end of Craig Daw, a long low crag close to the left bank of the water, which was the breeding place of the Hen Harrier and of the Kite, the latter better known locally as the Glentanner Gled. Eagles also breed in the glen. There are no dwelling houses above the mansion house, except Etnach, a forester's residence. The farm farthest up was at Coire-bhruach, where the Tanner is crossed by the Fir Mounth path, leading over Mount Keen to Glen Mark and Glen Esk. About a quarter of a mile above the ruins of the steading of Coirebhruach, seven miles above the mansion house, the carriage road ends at a neat little modern "shiel". Fully a mile farther up, at a height of about 2000 feet, on the right bank of Allt Deas, one of the head streams of the Tanner, is a fine corrie locally known as the "Slate Quarry". The origin of this name is unascertainable, but the place is as unlike a slate quarry as possibly can be. Considerable portions of the sides of the corrie are vertical to a height of over 300 feet, and are composed of pure white quartz, embedded in which may be observed numerous specimens of crystals. Manganese in some quantity is also found by Allt Deas.

Glen Tanner was formerly famed for its firs. The forest was twice burned last century, once it is believed by accident. An oak ship entirely made from timber grown in the glen was built at Aberdeen, and named the "Countess of Aboyne". The glen was, moreover, notorious for its smugglers, no fewer than fourteen smuggling bothies frequently working at one time, the manufactured article being regularly sent Brechin-wards in small barrels on horseback. Traces of smuggling bothies may still be observed, as well as of the huts of the workmen employed during the clearance long ago of the far-famed trees of the glen. The old distillers are without successors, but the pines, renewed and protected, still adorn the hill sides.

Mount Keen forms an excellent mountain excursion from Aboyne. Coirebhruach reached, a hill-track leads almost to the summit, a well-defined cone—the most Easterly hill-top over 3000 feet in Scotland. It is thus described by the Queen, who crossed it in 1861 in her "Second Great Expedition": "Mount Keen was in great beauty before us, and as we came down to Coirebhruach and looked down Glen Tanner, the scenery was grand and wild. Mount Keen is a curious conical-shaped hill, with a deep corrie [Corrach] in it . . . We came in sight of a new country, and looked down a very fine glen—Glen Mark. We descended by a very steep but winding path, called the Ladder, very grand and wild". An inscribed stone marks the spot, a little above the mansion house of Glentanner, where Her Majesty lunched on 21st September, 1861, on the return journey, *via* Cairn O' Mount.

The broom and whin, by loch and linn,
Are tipped wi' gowd in simmer weather,
Sweet and fair, but meikle mair,
The purple bells o' Hielan' heather.

Birse.

The name Birse is derived from the Gaelic *Preis*, and signifies a wooded country—a very proper appellation for the district. It is mainly drained by three streams flowing in a North-easterly direction, the Burn of Cattie, having Glen Cat in the upper part, the Water of Feugh, and the Water of Aven. The common expression, "As auld's the hills o' Birse", is held by some to refer, not to mountains, but to a family "Hill", the members of which lived to great ages.

Birsemore Hill and Craigendinnie are two hills on the opposite side of the Dee from Aboyne, separated by the Aulddinnie Burn, along which there is a track, sometimes called the Cateran Road, to the Forest of Birse and the upper part of the Feugh, leading on, between the head streams of the Tarf, to Glen Esk. The gorge is known as the Fungle, and, crowded as it is with firs, is a favourite resort of visitors. The late Sir William C. Brooks constructed a "Rest and be Thankful", and cut a gap in the trees, so that a view may be had of Aboyne and vicinity. The old mansion house of the estate of Birsemore lay on the North-eastern slope of the hill; its site can be traced with difficulty. It belonged to a branch of the Gordons of Cluny about the middle of the 15th century. In the 12th century Birse was the seat of the Chancellor of the Diocese of Aberdeen, and in later years Birsemore was one of the numerous summer residences of the Bishops.

About two miles East of the bridge of Aboyne the church of Birse is reached, near the left bank of the Burn of Birse. It dates from 1779, and is a rather plain building. When the foundations of the previous church, which stood a little to the South, were removed, a granite stone was found having a representation of a two-handed sword, a battle-axe, and a cross, probably dating from the 14th or 15th century. It is now built into the South wall of the churchyard. The burial place of the Farquharsons of Finzean is on the site of the old church.

The Rev. Alexander Gordon, Minister of Birse, translated from Kinerny, died in 1777, after a ministry in Birse of 51 years. Besides being a preacher and scholar of no mean attainments, he was also a noted violinist, and bore the sobriquet of "the fule fiddler o' Kinerny". The tune "Jenny dang the Weaver" was his composition. There is a monument to his memory in the South wall of the church. The Rev. George Knowles, of poetic fame, was his successor. He was a composer also, the tune "Birse", sometimes called "Balfour", being his composition.

The estate of Balfour, lying to the South of the church, belonged at one time to a branch of the Farquharsons of Finzean, and latterly to the Marquis of Huntly, who sold it, in 1840, to Mr. F. J. Cochran, the builder of the present mansion house. The Rev. John Skinner, the author of "Tullochgorum", was the son of a schoolmaster of Birse who had married the widow of Donald Farquharson of Balfour.

The mansion house of Ballogie is a fine large modern building on the left bank of the Burn of Cattie. In 1650 the estate of Ballogie, the ancient name of which was Tillysnaught, belonged to a branch of the Roses of Kilravock. It passed afterwards to a Forbes, and then to the Inneses of Balnacraig and their relations the Farquharsons, who sold it to Mr. James Dyce Nicol, at one time M.P. for Kincardineshire.

The estates and proprietors in the parish of Birse are: Birse, Joseph R. Heaven; Finzean, Dr. Robert Farquharson, M.P.; Ballogie and Midstrath, William E. Nicol; Balfour (part of), Trustees of the late Alexander Cochran; and Balfour (part of), Mrs.

Cochran. The Crown still owns the right of salmon fishing in the Dee in the Forest of Lendrum, letting the same to the proprietors of Finzean and Ballogie.

Tarland.

The village of Tarland is about 6 miles North-west from Aboyne. The Tarland road diverges from the North turnpike a little beyond the 31st mile-stone, and generally keeps pretty near the right bank of Tarland Burn. Passing Aboyne Castle on the right, with Queen's Hill and Mortlich Hill, the Vale of Cromar, with the church of Tarland, opens to view, bounded on the East, North, and West by an almost unbroken range of hills. Cromar was formerly considered one of the most fertile glens in Aberdeenshire; at one time it is believed that the greater portion was a lake, the waters being confined by a bar of high ground where the Aboyne road enters the Vale. It was held in early times by the Earls of Mar and the Durwards, whose names are so frequently met with on Deeside. On a green knoll, a little to the South of the church of Coull, close to the left bank of Tarland Burn, are the remains of the Castle of Coull, a stronghold of the Durwards. The importance of the Durwards in these parts is indicated by the tradition that the church bell of Coull rang of itself when a member of the family died. Alan, the greatest of the Durwards, and the last male descendant, died in 1272. The castle, said to have been built in 1115, was fifty yards square, and had five turrets. It was inhabited at the commencement of the 17th century, but became a ruin before its close. In 1798 there were three sides standing, but its utter demolition was hastened by the credulous, who expected to find gold under its broad walls; the materials at least were valuable for building farm steadings! The Earls of Mar, who owned the Southern and Western sides and indeed the greater part of Cromar, had their castle at Migvie; it may still be traced on a knoll near the church. Nearly opposite the church of Coull a road branches off to the right, leading to the Slack of Tillylodge on the water-shed between Deeside and Donside, the Eastern, and, before the Deeside Railway was constructed, the principal entrance to Cromar. In 1485 the lands of Tarland belonged to Sir John Rutherford of Migvy, Provost of Aberdeen, who sold them to Alexander Irvine of Drum in 1496; they were held by the Irvines for about 200 years, when they were purchased by the Earl of Aberdeen, now proprietor of most of the land near the village and Eastwards to the Slack of Tillylodge. There is no mansion; but the farm-house at Indego, about a mile East of the village, has been converted into a shooting-box, now known as Tarland Lodge. The church of Tarland was dedicated to Saint Maluack, and, together with Migvie, was gifted by the Earl of Mar in 1165 to the Priory of Saint Andrews. The Priors looked well after their rights, for, as an agreement dated 1222 shews, they exacted one pound annually from one of their vassals for "leave to be with Lord James, son of the late Morgund, Earl of Mar". The present church, built in 1870, contains a stained glass window to the memory of the late Lieut-Colonel John Farquharson of Corrachree in the neighbouring parish of Logie-Coldstone; the spire, built in 1889, was erected in memory of his widow. Among the antiquities of the district may be mentioned the remains of a Druidical circle on Tamnaverie, a small hill near the farm-house of Mill of Wester Coull, and Erde houses at Crossfold, Coull (a very well preserved specimen), at Culsh, about two miles East of the village of Tarland, and at Milltown of Migvie. The old parish of Migvie lies to the West of Tarland—the church being about three miles from the village—and was joined to that of Tarland, in 1618, under the name of Tarland-Migvie. At the church of Migvie is an unlettered stone, said to be that at which meetings were convened, and referred to in old records, where the Lord Superior summoned his vassals three times a year "*apud lapidem de Migveth*".

The village of Tarland was at one time of considerable importance in the locality, and even yet, though with somewhat decaying appearance, may be regarded as the "capital" of the district of Cromar, from the markets still held there and the business transacted. The smuggling of whiskey was carried on to a great extent in Tarland, as in other places on upper Deeside, during the last century and part of the present. The description "Roch Tykes o' Tarland" would appear to do but justice to the habits of the natives in those days.

The estates and proprietors in the parishes of Coull and Tarland are: Coull—Aberdeen, Earl of Aberdeen, John Sinclair, and James Charles Barclay Harvey; Coull, Alexander Riddell; O'Neil Corse, Trustees of the Hon. James O. Forbes; Aboyne, Trustees of the Marquis of Huntly; Finzean, Dr. Robert Farquharson, M.P.; and Craigievar, Trustees of Lord Sempill; Tarland—Cromar, Earl of Aberdeen; Corrachree and Drummie, Col. Sir John Farquharson,

K.C.B.; Ranna (part of) and Melgum, John A. Milne; Douneside, Alexander McRobert; and Ranna (part of), George Gellie.

THE EARL OF ABOYNE.

1. The Earl o Aboyne to old England's gone,
   An a his nobles wi him;
   Sair was the heart his fair lady had
   Because she wanna wi him.

2. As she was walking in her garden green,
   Amang her gentlewomen,
   Sad was the letter that came to her,
   Her lord was wed in Lunan.

3. 'Is this true, my Jean,' she says,
   'My lord is wed in Lunan?'
   'O no, O no, my lady gay,
   For the Lord o Aboyne is comin.'

4. When she was looking oer her castell-wa,
   She spied twa boys comin:
   'What news, what news, my bonny boys?
   What news hae ye frae Lunan?'

5. 'Good news, good news, my lady gay,
   The Lord o Aboyne is comin;
   He's scarcely twa miles frae the place,
   Ye'll hear his bridles ringin.'

6. 'O my grooms all, be well on call,
   An hae your stables shinin;
   Of corn an hay spare nane this day,
   Sin the Lord o Aboyne is comin.

7. 'My minstrels all, be well on call,
   And set your harps a tunin,
   Wi the finest springs, spare not the strings,
   Sin the Lord o Aboyne is comin.

8. ‘ My cooks all, be well on call,
An had your spits a runnin,
Wi the best o roast, an spare nae cost
Sin the Lord o Aboyne is comin.

9. ‘ My maids all be well on call,
An hae your flours a shinin :
Cover oer the stair wi herbs sweet an fair,
Cover the flours wi linen,
An dress my bodie in the finest array,
Sin the Lord o’ Aboyne is comin.’

10. Her gown was o the guid green silk,
Fastned wi red silk trimmin ;
Her apron was o the guid black gaze,
Her hood o the finest linen.

11. Sae stately she stept down the stair,
To look gin he was comin ;
She called on Kate, her chamber-maid,
An Jean her gentlewoman,
To bring a bottle of the best wine,
To drink his health that’s comin.

12. She’s gaen to the close, taen him frae’s horse,
Says, ‘ You’r thrice welcome frae Lunan !’
‘ If I be as welcome hauf as ye say,
Come kiss me for my comin,
For to-morrow should been my wedding-day
Gin I’de staid on langer in Lunan.’

13. She turned about wi a disdainful look
To Jean her gentlewoman :
‘ If tomorrow should been your wedding-day
Go kiss your miss in Lunan.’

14. ‘ O my nobles all, now turn your steeds,
I’m sorry for my comin ;
For the night we’ll alight at the bonny Bog o Gight,
Tomorrow tak horse for Lunan.’

15\. ‘ O Thomas, my man, gae after him,
An spier gin I'll win wi him ;’
‘ Yes, madam, I hae pleaded for thee,
But a mile ye winna win wi him.’

16\. Here and there she ran in care,
An Doctors wi her dealin ;
But in a crack her bonny heart brak,
And letters gaed to Lunan.

17\. When he saw the letter sealed wi black,
He fell on's horse a weeping :
‘ If she be dead that I love best,
She has my heart a keepin.

18\. ‘ My nobles all, ye'll turn your steeds,
That comely face I may see then ;
Frae the horse to the hat, a' must be black,
And mourn for bonny Peggy Irvine.’

19\. When they came near to the place,
They heard the dead-bell knellin,
And aye the turnin o the bell
Said, Come bury bonny Peggy Irvine.*

---

* Professor Child gives twelve versions of this ballad from manuscript and published sources. None of these dates further back than 1800, though Mrs. Brown of Falkland mentions it (23 Dec., 1800) as being sung when she was a child (in Aberdeenshire). The text here given is Child's "B" version from Buchan's "Gleanings of Scarce old Ballads," 1825, and the Gibb MS. (substantially the same as in Robertson's "Deeside Guide")—probably the earliest and best text.

"Charles, first Earl of Aboyne, married for his first wife Margaret Irvine of Drum, who died in December, 1662." *Records of Aboyne*, p. 552. "In Vol. ii. of *Retours* or Services of Heirs, No. 4906 (Aberdeen) 17 June, 1665, there is the entry—Domina Anna Gordonn, hæres Dominæ Margaretæ Irving, spousæ Comitis de Aboyne matris. The story of the ballad, as far as is known, is an absolute fiction." (Child's Ballads, v., p. 301.) Music: Christie's "Ballad Airs," i., p. 22.

LORD ABOYNE.

1. ‘ Aft hae I played at the ring and the ba’,
   And lang was a rantin’ lassie ;
   But now my father does me forsake,
   And my friends they all do neglect me.

2. But gin I had servants at my command,
   As I hae had right mony ;
   For to send awa’ to Glentanner’s yetts
   Wi’ a letter to my rantin’ laddie.

3. ‘ O, is your true love a laird or lord ?
   Or is he a highland caddie ;
   That ye sae aften call him by name,
   Your bonny, bonny rantin’ laddie ?’

4. ‘ My true love he’s baith laird and lord,
   Do ye think I hae married a caddie ?
   O he is the noble Earl o’ Aboyne,
   And he’s my bonny rantin’ laddie.’

5. ‘ O ye’se hae servants at your command,
   As ye hae had right mony ;
   For to send awa’ to Glentanner’s yetts
   Wi’ a letter to your rantin’ laddie.’

6. When Lord Aboyne the letter got,
   Wow, but he blinket bonny ;
   But ere three lines o’ it he read,
   O but his heart was sorry.

7. His face it redenned like a flame,
   He grasped his sword sae massy ;
   ‘ O wha is this dare be sae bauld,
   Sae cruel to use my lassie ?

8. ‘ Gae saddle to me five hundred men,
   Gae saddle and make them ready
   Wi’ a milk white steed under every ane,
   For I’m ga’ing to bring hame my lady.’

9. And when they came to auld Fedderate,
He found her waiting ready;
And he brought her to Castle Aboyne,
And now she's his ain dear lady.*

---

*From Buchan's "Ballads of the North of Scotland," 1828, vol. ii., p. 66. The earliest version of this ballad was that communicated by Burns with the music to Johnson's "Musical Museum" in 1797. It is substantially the same as the above except the opening verse, and of course different place names. Professor Child gives four traditionary versions, but adopts Burns and Buchan for his "A" text. A copy spun out by needless repetitions to 27 stanzas is given in Laing's "Thistle of Scotland," 1823. Music: Johnson's "Musical Museum," No. 462. R. A. Smith, "Scottish Minstrel," iv., p. 6. Christie's "Ballad Airs," i., p. 210.

IX.—ABOYNE TO BALLATER.

I.—By Rail and the North Road.

Look, oh look, from the bower!—'tis the beautiful hour
When the sunbeams are broad ere they sink in the sea;
Look, oh look, from the bower!—for an amethyst shower
Of glory and grandeur is gemming the Dee!

THE North road, the railway, and the river run closely together between Aboyne and Ballater. On leaving Aboyne station the railway passes through a short tunnel so as not to interfere with the amenities of the village. The road is interesting most of the way, and one feels that if not now actually in the Highlands, the gate, at least, is being opened. Into the subject of cairns, tumuli, and such like marks of bygone times, it is not for such a work as the present to enter to any extent; indeed, it would require a volume to itself, for, as one writer says, "cairns and tumuli are to be found on every hill and moor in the parish" of Aboyne, and indeed in the district. This is especially the case with the Muir of Dinnet, along which the tourist has now to pass, and the hills, small and great, that everywhere meet the view.

Ferrar will be passed on the right, three miles West from Aboyne. Here the first Earl of Sutherland was born; his father was Adam Gordon, the second son of the second Earl of Huntly. North-westward is Mullach Hill (919 feet), crowned with Mullach's Cairn, traditionally marking the spot where a Danish King or General of that name fell. Braeroddach, which was held by the Bissets for some time after Aboyne was lost to them, lies about three quarters of a mile to the North of Ferrar. A chapel formerly existed here, the ruins of which can still be traced. Near by is Braeroddach Loch, some 60 acres in extent, a noted breeding place for swans and other wild fowl.

Near the 34th mile-stone the river takes a short bend to the North. Half-way between the 34th and 35th mile-stones the Burn of Dinnet is crossed, and we enter the united parishes of Glenmuick-Tullich-Glengairn. A few yards beyond the 35th mile-stone Dinnet station is reached, and we are on what is accounted the Eastern border of the Deeside Highlands.

> Oh ! placid lake, could'st thou reflect
> The scenes that passed upon thy shore,
> When belted knights and warriors bold
> Assembled round the brave Canmore.

Dinnet.

Dinnet station is 4½ miles from Aboyne and 37 by rail from Aberdeen. Both the parish (*quoad sacra*) and the village, small as yet, may be said to owe their existence to the railway. The church is situated on the South side of the railway, and the village on the North. Tarland is distant 5 miles; Coldstone, 5 miles; and Boltinstone, 9¾ miles. The station is conveniently situated for some parts of upper Donside. A little to the West of the station is Dinnet House, the mansion of the estates of Kinord and Cromar. Since the extension of the railway to Ballater, a road has been made from the Dee Northward, crossing the railway at the station and leading on to Tarland and Donside. On the South side of the Dee there is a road leading over the ridge to Glen Tanner. The old ford below the present bridge was anciently guarded by a fort, traces of which are yet visible, and the name Dinnet may be derived from *dun* (a fortification) and *ath* (a ford).

Loch Kinord and Loch Davan, which are naturally drained by the Burn of Dinnet, though the greater portion of the outflow of the former has lately been diverted and utilised for the electric lighting of Dinnet House, are a little to the North-west of the station, the former being close to the North side of the road. Loch Kinord covers an area of about 225 acres, while Loch Davan, a quarter of a mile to the North, is of somewhat less extent. Both lochs are in the old parish of Tullich, now united to Glenmuick, with the exception of the North-east border of Loch Davan, which lies in Logie-Coldstone. Culblean Hill (1567 feet), a shoulder of Morven (2862 feet), slopes down to their Western shores, sending the Vat Burn to Loch Kinord. These lochs and the district in their immediate vicinity form, to antiquarians, one of the most interesting regions in the North of Scotland. The traces of pre-historic buildings and the "finds" shew unmistakably that there had, at a very early date, existed here a very important settlement and stronghold. The name Davan and other circumstances have induced the belief that this was the site of the Roman *Devana*. Many valuable "finds" have been made, comprising articles of stone, bronze, iron and timber. Among the latter are oak piles of a crannog and drawbridge, and several canoes. The late Sir William C. Brooks erected a beautiful little building, on the South shore of Loch Kinord, as a museum for preserving these and other antiquarian objects; but unfortunately, when his personal connection with the spot ceased, difficulties were placed by the then landowner in the way of the proper use of the interesting collection. There are several prettily wooded islets, some of them artificial, on Loch Kinord, the largest one having been the site of a castle, ascribed by tradition to Malcolm Canmore, while on another was a tolbooth. Edward I. and his army, as historic documents still shew, twice encamped a night in the Muir of Dinnet, the king himself, likely enough, staying in the castle on the loch. James IV. also passed at least a couple of nights in the castle in 1504. The battle of Culblean was fought in 1335 between the forces of David II., son of the Bruce, and those of Baliol, the latter commanded by the Earl of Athole. Baliol's army was completely routed, and the cairns, so numerous in the neighbourhood, doubtless cover the slain in this and earlier conflicts. Athole was slain, but some of his forces found shelter in the Castle Island. The site of the battle, minutely described by Wyntoun, is on the Eastern slope of Culblean and the West shore of Loch Davan. Reference should be made to Rev. J. G. Michie's "Loch Kinord" (1877), and "History of Logie-Coldstone and Braes of Cromar" (1896).

"The Vat" is about three-quarters of a mile West from Loch Kinord, and will repay a passing visit. It is a sort of cave in the course of the burn of that name, formed by rocks, the shape of which has suggested the name "Vat". A few trees in the crevices of the rocks add to their picturesqueness. "The Vat" is sometimes called Rob Roy's Cave, but it never had any connection with that notorious Highlander. A freebooter of the same clan, but of much less dignity, named Gilderoy, frequented it, and it is probably from this circumstance that the Macgregor's name has been coupled with "The Vat". Morven, the highest hill we have yet reached on the North side of the Dee in our Westward journey, is frequently ascended from Dinnet.

CHARLIE MACPHERSON.

1. Charlie MacPherson, that braw Hieland laddie,
On Valentine's even cam doun on Kinaldie,
Courtit Burd Hellen, baith wakin an sleepin;
'O, fair fa them has my love in keepin!'

2. Charlie MacPherson cam doun the dykeside,
Baith Milton an Muirton an a' bein his guide;
Baith Milton and Muirton an auld Wattie Nairn
A' gaed wi him, for to be his warn.

3. Whan he cam to the hoose o Kinaldie,
'Open your yetts, mistress, an lat us come in!
Open your yetts, mistress, an lat us come in!
For here's a commission come frae your gude son.

4. 'Madam,' says Charlie, 'whare is your dochter?
Mony time have I come to Kinaldie an socht her:
Noo maun she goe wi me mony a mile,
Because I've brocht mony men frae the West Isle.'

5. 'As for my dochter, she has gane abroad,
You'll no get her for her tocher gude;
She's on to Whitehouse, to marry auld Gairn:
Oh, fair fa them that wait on my bairn!'

6. Charlie MacPherson gaed up the dykeside,
Baith Muirton an Milton an a' bein his guide;
Baith Muirton an Milton an auld Wattie Nairn,
A' gaed wi him, for to be his warn.

7. When he cam to the hoose in Cromar,
Sae weel as he kent that his Nellie was there!
An Nellie was sittin upon the bed-side,
An every one there was ca'ing her, bride.

8. The canles gaed oot, they waurna weel licht,
Swords an spears they glancet fou bricht;
Sae laith as she was her true-love to beguile,
Because he brocht mony men frae the West Isle.*

. . . .

Logie-Coldstone.

The parish of Logie-Coldstone occupies the South and West sides of the Vale of Cromar, extending from Loch Kinord to Deskrie Burn (a tributary of the Don), and including a large portion of Morven. The principal access is from Dinnet, the road from which traverses its greatest length, to Boltinstone, about 8 miles. On the right or Eastern side of this road, in the centre of a great moss near Dinnet station, may be seen buildings for

* The text of this fragmentary ballad is from the Harris MS. in Harvard University Library, and was taken down from the singing of Mrs. Harris, who learned it in Perthshire at the end of last century. It is sung to the air, "Whilk o ye lasses." It is printed in Child's "English and Scottish Popular Ballads," vol. iv., p. 309. The ballad was also known to Mrs. Brown of Falkland, who mentions in a letter to A. F. Tytler (23rd December, 1800), "The carrying-off of the Heiress of Kinady," as among other Aberdeenshire ballads still in her memory. Buchan, "Ballads of The North of Scotland," gives a very tame version of this ballad—Charlie returning to his "West Isle" leaving his lass to marry "auld Gairn." We have corrected the proper names *Kinaltie*; *Kinatie*;—*Braemar*; *Watter*;—to *Kinaldie*; *Cromar*; *Wattie*; as in Buchan's text. The Kinaldie here referred to is in the parish of Logie-Coldstone, Cromar; and Whitehouse lies about a mile to the south of Kinaldie.

the manufacture of a diatomaceous deposit of great extent, discovered here in 1876 by Rev. George Davidson, minister of the parish. It is dug like peat from under the moss, is of a greyish colour, and when dried becomes light and spongy. It is then burned in a specially prepared furnace, which gives it a chalky appearance. It is used largely as an absorbent of nitro-glycerine, and in polishing and dyeing preparations. On the Northern margin of the moss is Ordie, a good specimen of the old Highland clachan, which passed, our road is crossed by the Tarland and Braemar road. A finger-post here gives the following distances: Coldstone, 2¾ miles; Dinnet, 2¼ miles; Ballater, 7¾ miles; Tarland, 2¾ miles. About a mile farther Westward an entrance gate to Blelack House is passed, near which is Currae Hillock, on the top of which is a curious hollow which, according to legend, was a great "Howff" of the fairies. Half-a-mile Southward is the old burial ground, still in use, of Logie-Mar; the church was dedicated to St. Wallock. There is a stone at the gate still known as St. Wallock's Stone—probably that at which Head Courts were convened and justice administered. His name is also commemorated by a Fair, the date of which was observed as a holiday after the Market had ceased to exist:

> Saint Wallock's Fair in Logie-Mar
> On the thirtieth day of Januar.

The church was gifted to the Priory of Monymusk by Gilchrist, Earl of Mar, about 1200; but his successor, Duncan (1239-44), withdrew this grant and gave it to the Bishop of Aberdeen, under condition that his body should be interred at St. Machar's Cathedral. There are some old and interesting epitaphs in the churchyard. Here, within the Blelack Howff, the Gordons, who were lairds of Blelack for over 200 years, are interred. The last laird was "out in the '45", and his consequent misfortunes, the forfeiture of his estate and the destruction of his house, were by some attributed to the fairies' malediction:

> Dool, dool to Blelack,
>   And dool to Blelack's heir,
> For drivin' us frae the Seely Howe,
>   To the cauld Hill o' Fare!

These Gordons figured largely in the history of the district during the 17th and 18th centuries. The lands were sold in 1802 to John Forbes of Newe, and again in 1862 to Sir Alexander Anderson, Lord Provost of Aberdeen; in 1869 they were purchased by the present proprietor, Mr. William B. Coltman. Near Blelack House are Poldhu Wells, which were formerly believed to possess medicinal properties.

The parishes of Logie-Mar and Coldstone, the old name of which was Hàchagoward, were conjoined in 1618, and the united parish named Logie-Coldstone. The church is at Newkirk, a name adopted after the church for the combined parishes was built. Here there is another finger-post: Dinnet, 4½ miles; Ballater, 9 miles; Cross Road, ¾ mile; Tillypronie, 3¾ miles; Boltinstone, 4¾ miles.

The church of Coldstone stood at one time within the churchyard, which is beautifully situated, about half-a-mile Northward, on the Southern slope of a tree-clad hill whence, to the South, Mount Keen stands out cone-like, to the West Morven, while to the East the obelisk on Mortlich will just be seen. Alexander Laing, the author of the *Caledonian Itinerary*, *Donean Tourist*, &c., is interred here. He was born in Coull, and died at Boltinstone in 1838. The site of the old church may be traced; there is a small stone of apparently great antiquity, on which is cut a cross within an oval, said to be of Culdee character. An Erde house was recently discovered on the farm of Whitehouse, and there are numerous prehistoric remains in the district, apparently of human habitations, in groups or villages. Some may yet be seen near Knocksoul.

After passing the manse and old burial ground of Coldstone, the road is joined by the Tarland and Strathdon road at the entrance gate to Tillypronie House (Sir John F. Clark, Bart.). The house is situated on the Eastern slope of a hill from which there is a magnificent view of the whole Vale of Cromar, as well as of other parts of Deeside. At the entrance gate a direction-post gives the following distances: Coldstone, 2 miles; Dinnet, 6½ miles; Ballater, 11 miles; Tarland, 4½ miles; Aboyne, 10 miles; Boltinstone, 2¼ miles.

> Wo to the day John Tam was married,
> Culblean was burn'd, and Cromar was harried.

The district of Cromar, according to Sir James Balfour's Collections, consists of the ancient parishes of Logie-Mar, Coldstone, Migvie, Tarland, and Coull. The couplet just quoted refers to Mackay's visitation with fire and sword after the battle of Killiecrankie.

The estates and proprietors in Logie-Coldstone are: Cromar (part of), Earl of Aberdeen; Glendavan,

Alexander Ogston, M.D.; Cromar (part of) and Kinord, James Charles Barclay Harvey; Blelack and Deskrie, William B. Coltman; Corrachree, Colonel Sir John Farquharson, K.C.B.; Hopewell, Duncan Robertson; Melgum, John A. Milne; Aboyne, Trustees of the Marquis of Huntly; Finzean, Dr. Robert Farquharson, M.P.; and Tillypronie, Marriage Trustees of Sir John F. Clark, Bart.

Yet ne'er in your roaming, from morn-break till gloaming,
Shall scene more endearing e'er lighten the way,
Than where the Dee gliding, through beauty abiding,
Salutes with soft murmur sweet Cambus o' May.

Cambus o' May.

The station of Cambus o' May, 2½ miles Westward from Dinnet, is typically Highland, being situated on a rocky hill side among fir trees, with heather growing along the platform. The river runs so close that one might almost fish from the carriage windows! Granite quarries have been opened on the rocky hill slopes on the North side of the road, producing excellent stone. Here one feels in the Highlands; the tameness of lowland scenery is now completely left behind. Looking Westward the glorious mountain view is entrancing—Lochnagar, the Coyles of Muick, Craigendarroch and other less known hills of great beauty. Nor is the prospect across the Dee—here forming a bend which gives name to the station—less pleasant, with Ballaterach and the basin of the Pollagach Burn in the foreground. The tourist, ere he has reached this point, will have admitted that the charms of Deeside are equal to their reputation. "The trees here", says the inimitable "James Brown" in his *New*

Deeside Guide (1842), "are thought to have few equals on Deeside. What is very curious, is that, when the great floods of August, 1829, had abated, there was found within the bench or plate rack [of a small inn here] a full-grown trout, which no doubt had swam in here, where it was doomed to die a miserable death. This may serve to show how high the waters rose in that cruel and terrible flood". This old wayside hostelry is still in existence—as a dwelling-house; the building is a few yards West of the station, and so close to the South side of the railway, that it was necessary to shave off a corner of the house.

About a mile West from the station a birch-clad knoll will be passed on the left, surmounted by a high slender obelisk of Aberdeen granite, erected in memory of William Farquharson of Monaltrie, who died on 20th November, 1828. His uncle was Francis Farquharson, the "Baron Ban", who fought at the head of the Farquharsons at Culloden, where he was taken prisoner. At his subsequent trial he was condemned to death and his estates confiscated, but he was afterwards pardoned, and on payment of £1613 0s. 9d., received back his ancestral possessions.

Calm sleep the village dead,
In the auld kirk-yard;
But softly, slowly, tread
In the auld kirk-yard.

Tullich.

The church of Tullich was dedicated to St. Nathalan, Bishop of Aberdeen, who died in 452. The ruined church, which probably dates from about 1450, is in the churchyard, beside the 40th mile-stone, on the East side of Bridge of Tullich. In the 13th century the patronage was held by the Knights of St. John; the line of fortification made by them may still be traced. There are three sculptured stones at the church, the earliest of which is believed by Rev. J. G. Michie to be probably referable to the days of sun worship; the next is probably of Culdee origin; the most recent is of Roman Catholic times. Tullich was a vicarage, and its relative importance will be understood from the fact that the churches of Glenmuick and Glengairn belonged to it. The "barony of Tullich" is mentioned in the Exchequer Roll under date 1337; in 1484 Sir Symon Kingorne is named as "vicor of Tullyche". In 1552 the rental of the lands of Tullich is stated as "the mill annuelis with mill lands, one plough, 2 tenants' rents £5 6s. 8d., a wedder, a sow or 20s. (both Scots), 12 capons, and the leit of peats". Nathalan, for a penance, according to tradition, locked an iron girdle around his loins and threw the key into the Dee at a place still known as the "Key Pool", a little to the South-west of the church. Thereafter he set out for Rome, where in a fish that was brought him by an Italian fisherman he duly found the key, which he received as a sign that his sins were forgiven. This legend is also prettily connected with a great famine in Deeside, during which Nathalan, having sown his fields with sand, had an abundant crop of corn. When he began, with the assistance of his parishioners, to harvest the heaven-sent grain, a sudden storm threatened to damage it, on which Nathalan forgot himself, and grumbled, like an ordinary farmer, at the weather. In a moment all was again fair, but with this fresh evidence of divine interposition Nathalan felt his own utter unworthiness; and so, locking a chain round his ankle, he threw away the key. The rest we know. The famous Reel of Tullich is said to have been composed, in the church, on a certain cold stormy Sunday, when the priest failed to put in an appearance, though not an inconsiderable number of his parishioners assembled, and passed the time of waiting and also warmed themselves by dancing. The burial aisle of the Farquharsons of Whitehouse is within the walls of the church.

Tomnakiest may be observed, in the neighbourhood of the granite quarries, about a mile to the Eastward of the church of Tullich. The farm has been continuously in the occupation of the Sandison family for over four centuries.

When I roved a young Highlander o'er the dark heath,
And climbed thy steep summit, O Morven of snow,
To gaze on the torrent that thundered beneath,
Or the mist of the tempest that gathered below.

Morven.

The Burn of Tullich, which the road crosses a few yards West of the ruined kirk, rises on Morven, and, rushing through a deep narrow gorge between Creagan Riach (1600 feet) on the West and Crannach Hill (1824 feet) on the East, enters the Dee opposite Pannanich. A path along the right bank of the burn is the usual route from Ballater to the summit, the Blue Cairn, of Morven. The view is very fine: Lochnagar looks by far the best of the mountains visible, though the Eastern Cairngorms have a grand appearance, and Mount Keen and Bennachie are particularly noticeable. Morven was ascended by the Queen on 14th September, 1859. Viewed from the South it has rather a conical shape, while from the Eastward it presents a massive but graceful outline. The mountain consists of hornblende rock, and generally has a smooth, grassy surface.

The view of Ballater and its surrounding mountains from the neighbourhood of Bridge of Tullich is magnificent—one of the finest prospects on Deeside. A few yards West of the bridge the road forks—by the right through the Pass of Ballater to Braemar, and by the left to Ballater, rejoining the Braemar road East of Bridge of Gairn.

II.—By the South Road.

We'll up the muir o' Charlestown,
An' ower the water o' Dee,
An' hine awa' to Candecaill,
It's there whaur we should be.

The South road from Aboyne to Ballater is not without particular interest; it has a more distinctly Highland character than the fine modern turnpike on the left bank of the river. Crossing the Dee by the suspension bridge, and the Tanner by Bridge of Ess, the first object of interest passed is the ruined church of Glentanner, lying between the road and the river. Only the West gable remains, the East side of the wall being appropriated for a tombstone. The ancient building, like others in Deeside, was thatched with heather, and was known as the Black Kirk of the Moor. "Byron's Mary" is interred in the churchyard, her tombstone stating that she died in Aberdeen, on 2nd March, 1867, aged 85 years.

About a mile Westward from the ruined church is the Bridge of Dinnet, taking the place of a ferry a little lower down the river. The Manse of Dinnet is finely situated at the North-west end of the bridge.

Dee Castle is about two miles South-westward from Dinnet Bridge, on the South side of the road, just within the Glenmuick boundary, The old name was Candecaill (*Cean-na-coil* = Woodhead). Built by the first Marquis of Huntly, it was at one time the family residence on the Inchmarnoch portion of the Gordon estates, but little now remains of the old building, which was burned in 1641, the site being occupied by a small modern erection, overlooked by the hill of Little Tulloch. On this hill, according to *The New Statistical Account*, "are the remains of what is called 'My Lord's House'. . . . The use of this building is reported to have been for obtaining a view during a deer-hunt". Here the Earl of Mar met some of his friends after engaging with them in a deer-hunt in Glen Tanner, immediately previous to the rising of 1715. Thence they proceeded to Braemar. Inchmarnoch was at one time an independent parish, but long ago it became merged in Glenmuick. Its church and burial-ground can still be traced; the Dee has made an island on the site, and the flood of 1829 exposed several graves. The bell of the church had been suspended from a neighbouring tree, as was not uncommon in old times; Bellbrae, in the immediate vicinity, owes its name to this circumstance.

> Ballaterach's banks and sunny braes,
> I maun leave them a', lassie.

Little over a mile Westward from Dee Castle is Ballaterach, notable as the residence, for a short time, of

Lord Byron when a boy. One of the Huntly workmen, brought to assist at the building of Candecaill, was a Robertson, whose descendants found a home at Ballaterach, and of whose household the future poet, sent to the country on recovering from a fever, became temporarily a member. Here Byron met his "Mary", the second daughter of the family. Ballaterach has been much visited by admirers of Byron, and a wooden "box"-bed was long an object of interest, no less a sum than £40 having been offered for it, as it was generally believed to have been used by the future poet. It was accidently burned in 1868. The real bed was disposed of long before that date, being turned into a cheese-press at Dee Castle. At the neighbouring farm of Graystone the mistress of the house points out, with pride, several ash chairs, dating from last century, which had doubtless been used by Byron, who was a frequent caller at Graystone. He is said then to have had big prominent eyes, and to have been of a frolicsome disposition. The then tenant of Graystone, an ancestor of its present occupant, was a wheelwright, who, when he saw the boy approaching, took the precaution of closing his workshop! The neighbouring miller of Inchmarnoch had also to stop his mill when he appeared!

The Pollagach Burn joins the Dee near Ballaterach. Near its source it is crossed by the public path from Ballater to Mount Keen. A little above Ballaterach there is a ferry across the Dee to Cambus o' May. In this neighbourhood the growth of natural birch along the road is profuse and the perfume delightful.

Leaving Ballaterach, the hamlet and Wells of Pannanich will soon be reached, and presently we find

Ballater from Pannanich.

ourselves at Ballater Bridge, at the South end of which is a direction-post with the following information: Pannanich, 1¾ miles; Dinnet Bridge, 6½ miles; Aboyne, 11 miles; Glenmuick House, 1 mile; Abergeldie, 6¼ miles; Balmoral, 8½ miles. Pannanich Wells are said to have been accidentally "discovered" in 1760 by an old woman, who, full of scrofulous sores, bathed them in the scum of a bog. The result was as startling as pleasant, the cure became famous, and the bog developed into the "Wells". In 1793 a surgeon advertised in the *Aberdeen Journal* that he "will attend at the Wells every week, and will pay due attention to convalescents dispersed in different hamlets for the benefit of the goat milk". A writer in 1825 says, "none of them [the baths] is very inviting . . . The lower classes are extremely credulous respecting the medicinal virtues" of the Wells; and "groups of care-worn and sickly creatures, whose narrow funds excluded them from the bath-house, were patiently catching the water as it trickled over the discoloured stones on the open side of the hill". Some would "drink of a morning seven or eight quarts [! !] without feeling the least uneasiness . . . but in no case should the quantity exceed two Scottish pints".

X.—BALLATER.

Here hills aspire
To crown their heads with the æthereall fire:
Hills, bulwarks of our freedome, giant walls,
Which never fremdling's slight nor sword made thralls.

BALLATER, the Western terminus of the Deeside Railway, is 4 miles from Cambus o' May and 43½ from Aberdeen. The station is situated at the North-east corner of the burgh. Few provincial railway stations are more favoured with the arrival and departure of royal, noble, and important personages. The stranger, leaving the train at its final halt, and observing the mountains that confine the little plain of Ballater, almost threatening to overwhelm it, doubts no longer that the veritable Highlands of Scotland have been reached. The Westward prospect is sublime. The valley of the Dee is narrowed by pine-clad hills and bare mountain tops closing in on either bank. The gazing eye gets bewildered, so numerous, so varied, so wild withal, are the labyrinths of mountain scenery, stretching away towards the setting sun. Hills tower above hills, like the waves of a tempestuous sea suddenly arrested, with "Dark Lochnagar", ten miles to the South-west, rising high above them all.

Ballater is the capital of the Deeside Highlands, and is deservedly popular. During the season the village and neighbourhood are quite crowded with visitors from all parts of the country; while on holidays and Saturdays special trains are run for the accommodation of excursionists. It is 42 miles by road from Aberdeen, and is built on a fine meadow, at an altitude of about 700 feet above sea level, round which the Dee sweeps in a beautiful curve. The bold rock of Craigendarroch bounds it on the North-west; on the South-east is the river with Craig Coillach, a spur of Pannanich Hill (1896 feet); and while its natural attractions are numerous, it is also a good centre for "sight-seeing" and mountaineering, and a chosen resort of sportsmen. It is the main gateway to Braemar; Balmoral Castle, Abergeldie Castle, and Birkhall are within easy distances; three glens, Tullich, Muick, and Gairn, converge within a radius of a mile and a half; it is the popular base for the ascent of Lochnagar; by Mount Keen, Glen Esk may be reached; and by Glen Muick the Capel Mounth may be crossed *en route* for Glen Clova or Glen Doll. Donside may be reached over Morven, or by Glen Gairn and Glen Finzie, or by other routes. The Eastern Cairngorms and the basin of the Spey are also reached by Glen Gairn. Altogether it will be found a convenient starting or central point, alike for those who drive, walk, or cycle; for golfers there is also an excellent little course. Yet in 1760 the site of the village was a bare moor without a single house. In that year the little "capital" of the district was a village near the church of Tullich, and on the Wells of Pannanich becoming famous, the hamlet of Pannanich and the village of Ballater were built for the accommodation of those who flocked thither; in 1830 Ballater is described as "always crowded during the summer months with invalids and other visitors, brought together by the fame of the chalybeate wells of Pannanich and the magnificence and beauty of the surrounding scenery". Though the Wells have, like many others, lost their first reputation Pannanich is still much resorted to, and boasts of a visit by the Queen on 3rd October, 1870.

The burgh is yearly increasing, as convenient houses are built for the use of summer visitors. The Established Church stands in the "Square"; as also a (generally waterless) fountain presented by a former provost; and the Free Church is at the North-west end of the village. Close to the railway station are the Albert Memorial Hall, the Victoria Hall, and the Gordon Institute, with library and reading rooms, &c., presented to the inhabitants by the late Mr. Alexander Gordon, a native of the parish. The Barracks used by the guard of honour, when the Queen is at Balmoral Castle, are a little beyond the Free Church. Some of the best houses are to be found in Braemar Road, on the slope of Craigendarroch, where also there is a fine "Jubilee" fountain. A granite bridge gives access to the South side of the river. The famous flood of 4th August, 1829, carried away the then existing bridge, besides causing great havoc in the neighbourhood.

Craigendarroch (about 1300 feet) is the most interesting physical feature in the immediate vicinity of the village. It consists of red granite, craggy towards the summit, shaped like a huge mound, and wooded with oak, pine, birch, and aspen. From the top, on which two small guns were at one time mounted, a good view is got, the valley of the Dee being well seen, with Glen Gairn and Glen Muick. Without doubt the grandest object seen from Ballater is Lochnagar, with the Coyles of Muick in the foreground The famed Pass of Ballater is a deep, narrow gorge between Craigendarroch and Creag an t-Seabhaig, and forms an interesting feature of the landscape. The name "Ballater" is of some antiquity, for there is mention in the 15th century of "Balader", a little hamlet, long vanished, at the Eastern end of the Pass. Monaltrie House occupies a beautiful site at the foot of Craigendarroch, on the Western slope of which Craigendarroch Lodge, built of free-stone, replaces an older and smaller building of the same name.

The walks about Ballater may be summarised here for the convenience of excursionists. They are interesting and varied, and of length suitable for every kind of tourist. The old railway line may be mentioned first; it is entered opposite the Barracks, and is now an avenue of trees by the bank of the river for about a mile. It ends at Bridge of Gairn, whence the turnpike may be taken for the return journey. The path to the Pass of Ballater is entered on the North side of the station, passing Monaltrie House on the left and so joining the road at right angles, and turning to the left at the East end of the Pass. This road joins the Craigendarroch turnpike a short distance East of Bridge of Gairn, and so a little circular tour may be completed. The old church of Tullich may be made the goal, in which case, when the Pass is entered, as above, the turning is made to the right. The return journey may be made by the turnpike, taking the left fork near Milton of Tullich, and so entering the village at the hotel. A less-known but very fine circular walk may be had by going a little past Bridge of Gairn, where Polhollick foot-bridge crosses the Dee, then following a road to Bridge of Muick, and returning to the village by the South Deeside turnpike. Craig Coillach is one of the most popular resorts. Here the visitor may have rest on a warm day in the shade of the trees, as well as a fine view of the village, convenient seats being provided; while many take advantage of the path and so reach the cairn, where the prospect amply rewards the slight exertion necessary for such a moderate climb. The public are indebted to Sir Allan R. Mackenzie for the Craig Coillach facilities. The Wells of Pannanich, it may be noticed here, are within the ordinary pedestrian's range; for them the South road must of course be taken; the return may be slightly varied by keeping pretty close to the river bank for some distance after leaving the Wells. The view of Ballater and Craigendarroch from this point is exceedingly popular with artists.

Ballater, being the railway terminus, is a great centre for driving, and numerous pleasant excursions, circular and other, may thus be made: Balmoral—up the North road, down the South; Braemar; Glen Gairn and Loch Builg, returning by Balmoral; Glen Muick, Inschnabobart, and Balmoral—a circular drive; Loch Muick (Lochnagar, &c.); Falls of Muick; Mill of Stern; Pass of Ballater; Burn of the Vat; Bridge of Dinnet by the South road, returning by Loch Kinord; Glen Tanner—returning by Dinnet or Aboyne; and Donside (Corgarff, Castle Newe, &c.). There are usually circular excursions to Balmoral on Saturday afternoons during the season.

The principal estates and proprietors in the parish of Glenmuick-Tullich-Glengairn are: Glenmuick,

Testamentary Trustees of the late Sir James T. Mackenzie, Bart.; Invercauld and Monaltrie, Alexander H. Farquharson; Abergeldie, Hugh M. Gordon; Birkhall, Her Majesty the Queen; Glentana, *Sir William Cunliffe Brooks, Bart.*; Kinord, James Charles Barclay Harvey; Morven, Trustees of the late James M. Keiller; and Cambus o' May, Captain John F. Gaskell.

> Now turn I to that God of old,
> Who mocked not any of my ills,
> But gave my hungry hands to hold
> The large religion of the hills.

Glen Muick.

The Muick is one of the largest tributaries of the Dee, joining it on the right bank about half a mile above Ballater Bridge. It rises on Lochnagar, and, after a course of about two miles, flows into Dubh Loch, from which it emerges as Allt an Dubh-loch, and after another run of two miles enters Loch Muick, which it leaves as the Muick. About half-way between Loch Muick and the Dee is the picturesque Linn of Muick, a perpendicular cascade amid fine rock and thickly wooded scenery, at a point where the glen is considerably contracted. The Falls are much visited by tourists, and were famous even in Pennant's time, for he tells us that the pool was "supposed by the vulgar to be bottomless". On the left bank of the Muick are several noted places of interest—the Queen's Glasallt Shiel (on Loch Muick), Alltnagiubhsaich Lodge, and Birkhall; the ruined Knock Castle; and the churchyard of the parish of Glenmuick. On the right bank are Spital (the starting point for Capel Mounth), Glenmuick House, and Braichlie. Lochnagar partly drains to the left bank of the Muick in its upper part; lower down there are the Coyles of Muick, those beautiful green "miniature mountains", which are so much admired from Ballater and vicinity.

Starting from Ballater for Glen Muick the Dee is crossed at Ballater Bridge and the South road taken for a short distance. Braichlie House (Sir Allan R. Mackenzie, Bart.), near the site of the old castle of that name, will be passed on the left in about half a mile. A few yards above its junction with the Dee, the Muick is crossed by the South road at Bridge of Muick. A direction-post here gives the following distances: Falls of Muick, 5 miles; Loch Muick, 8½ miles; Birkhall, 1¾ miles; Balmoral, 7¾ miles. There is a driving road on each side of the Muick, from Lochend on the right bank and Glasallt Shiel on the left, but the greater part of the latter road is private, as it passes through the Queen's grounds. Leaving Bridge of Muick on the right, and keeping on the Mackenzie (Glenmuick) side of the glen, a handsome little Episcopal church, built by Sir J. T. Mackenzie in 1875, will soon be passed on the left. Close to it is a vault where are interred the remains of several members of the Mackenzie family, including those of the first baronet of Glenmuick. Glenmuick House occupies a commanding position. Built of granite in the Tudor style of architecture, the North, which is the principal elevation, has a handsome portico, with a covered-in carriage-way, surmounted by a massive-looking square tower 75 feet in height.

Birkhall will be observed on the opposite side of the river, and the Falls will be passed on the right, and afterwards, on emerging from the Linn Wood, which clothes the sides of the glen, a view of Lochnagar is obtained. At first the summit is not visible, but as Spital is neared the highest point comes into view with its "steep frowning glories". Spital of Muick was established at a very early date by the Bishop and Chapter of Aberdeen; in the fulness of time it was succeeded by a hostelry, the latter in its turn giving way to a forester's cottage. The driving road is continued for about a mile South from Spital to Lochend, a small shooting-box at the North-east end of Loch Muick. The Capel Mounth track branches off to the left shortly after leaving Spital. A pony path leads from Lochend along the loch-side to Black Burn, which enters Loch Muick near its upper end. Here the hill-slope, writes the Queen, "is very fine indeed, and deeply furrowed by the torrents, which form glens and corries where birch and alder trees grow close to the water's edge. We landed on a sandy spot below a fine glen, through which flows the Black Burn. It was very dry here, but still very picturesque, with alder trees and mountain ash in full fruit overhanging it". At the bridge over the burn the main path "takes the hill", crossing the county march to Bachnagairn, a disused shooting box on the South Esk, also on the Mackenzie property.

A rough path leads from Spital to Alltnagiubhsaich Lodge, crossing the Muick by a foot-bridge.

The other road from Bridge of Muick on the Balmoral side of the glen may be taken. The gate of the churchyard of Glenmuick is close to the North-west end of the bridge, where the old church, dedicated to the Virgin Mary, stood. In 1798 a new church was built in Ballater, and, strangely enough, on the night its foundation was laid, the old building at the bridge was burned. The burial-place of the Gordons of Abergeldie is in the churchyard, and is distinguished by a high obelisk within an iron railing. The most interesting slab, however, stands close to the entrance gate, and bears the following inscription very rudely cut: "1596 I. M.: 1722". The initials refer, it is believed, to a John Mitchell who lived at Dalliefour, about a mile to the North-west of the churchyard, the dates being the years of his birth and death respectively! Near the Western dyke of the churchyard there are several coffin-shaped slabs bearing initials and dates only; some are without even that meagre record, indicating that they must have been placed there when the art of cutting on granite was little known in Highland glens.

Proceeding along the South road a "Standing Stone", Scurry Stane, will be passed on the left, a little short of the 43rd mile-stone. Knock Castle will now be observed among trees a little to the West, on a hillock forming part of "The Knock", which rises within a bend of the Dee opposite the mouth of the Gairn. The castle, which probably dates from about 1600, replaced a tower which had stood for centuries near the same site, and which dated back to the times of the ancient Earls of Mar. At one time it was held by the Durwards, and was garrisoned to maintain the Royal authority on upper Deeside. Knock (along with Birkhall) ultimately came into the possession of the Gordons of Abergeldie, with whom it was a favourite seat, but they allowed it to become ruinous about a hundred years ago.

A few yards beyond the 43rd mile-stone the glen road leaves the South road and makes for the West side of the Muick. Birkhall, pleasantly situated among trees, will be passed on the left. Formerly part of the Abergeldie estate, it was purchased for the Prince of Wales, from whom Her Majesty acquired it and Alltnagiubhsaich Lodge. Although only a plain three-

Knock Castle.

story house, Birkhall is a delightful residence, and is generally "lent" by the Queen during the summer and autumn. The original front, which dates from 1715 and is ivy-clad, faces the Muick, but an addition, of the same height, faces Ballater. Mill of Stern, half a mile farther up, previous to the depopulation of the glen was a corn-mill, but is now a saw-mill. Above this point the road is "private", and there are several gates. Beyond the Falls the road, blasted from rock, runs closely by the stream, and is known as the Prince's Drive, so named from Prince Albert.

The Coyles of Muick are prominent objects on the Balmoral side of the glen. The highest peak attains a height of 1956 feet, and is surmounted by a cairn with the inscription: "Erected by command of Queen Victoria in Remembrance of the Marriage of Albert Edward Prince of Wales and Alexandra, Princess of Denmark, 10th March, 1863". The Coyles consist of serpentine with dykes of felspar, porphyry, and hornblende rocks (diorite), extending to Braichlie Burn, where granite succeeds.

After passing the Falls, Inschnabobart, a small farm about two miles below the loch, is the only cultivated ground. It is connected with the other side of the glen by a ford only. The great hollow containing Lock Muick has been in view for some time; about a mile short of the loch is pine-sheltered Alltnagiubhsaich Lodge, the "key" to Lochnagar from the Ballater side. The public path to the summit passes in rear of the Lodge, which was at one time known as "the Hut". A hundred years ago the "Hut" was a sod covered, one-chimneyed building; latterly it is described as "a most commodious cottage, belonging to Captain Gordon". The Lodge, which is now generally without an occupant, was frequently visited by the Queen and Prince Consort, when two or three days at a time would be spent under its roof, Her Majesty describing it as "our humble little abode". Here also, after a day among the stags on Lochnagar, the Prince of Wales and other members of the Royal Family have spent many a pleasant night, enlivened by a torch-light dance on the lawn. A direct carriage

Lochnagar—" The steep frowning glories".

road connects Balmoral Castle with Alltnagiubhsaich Lodge and Glassalt Shiel. On 7th October, 1863, the Queen rode over the Capel Mounth, and on the return from Alltnagiubhsaich the royal carriage was upset in the darkness near the head of Strath Girnock, not without injury to Her Majesty.

> England ! thy beauties are tame and domestic
> To one who has roved o'er the mountains afar :
> Oh for the crags that are wild and majestic !
> The steep frowning glories of dark Lochnagar !

Lochnagar is known wherever the English language is spoken or read, a fact for which three reasons may be adduced—the celebrity acquired through Byron's verses, the prominence given to it through the Queen's long residence under its shadow, and the sublimity of the mountain itself. It was long known as the White Mounth, as indeed its deer forest, the property of Her Majesty, is still called ; but the older name, Benchinnans—a corruption of Bin-chichin, "the mountain with the paps"—is, despite its appropriateness, almost forgotten. The highest point is named Cac Carn Beag (3786 feet), to the east of which, at an altitude of 2575 feet is the tarn, Lochnagar, "the goat's loch", which has extended its name, in modern times, to the mountain itself. Viewed from the East, North, or North-west, the outline of Lochnagar is particularly graceful, attracting attention from considerable distances. The Queen has made the ascent several times, and it is naturally a favourite climb with members of the Royal Family. (See the author's *Lochnagar*.)

Loch Muick lies at an altitude of 1310 feet, and is fully two miles in length, and about half a mile in breadth. Almost wholly enclosed by mountains, with steep declivities grooved by torrents, it impresses one by its solitude and grandeur. Trout are plentiful, and wild birds frequent its shores; even geese and swans may occasionally be seen in the vicinity. There is evidence that at some not very remote period the loch has been considerably longer; possibly has even extended to the Linn Wood. It is artistically described by the Queen: "The scenery is beautiful here, so wild and grand—real severe Highland scenery, with trees in the hollow. We had various scrambles in and out of the boat and along the shore, and saw three hawks, and caught seventy trout. I wish an artist could have been there to sketch the scene; it was so picturesque—the boat, the net, and the people in their kilts in the water and on the shore. . . . The moon rose, and was beautifully reflected on the loch, which, with its steep green hills, looked lovely. To add to the beauty, poetry, and wildness of the scene, Coutts played in the boat, the men giving an occasional shout when he played a reel". Glasallt Shiel, near the upper end of the loch, derives its name from the neighbouring Glas Allt, the falls of which, about 150 feet in height, are situated at the head of a deep, rocky gorge behind the Shiel. Built on a little tree-covered delta formed by the burn, it is the most remote and solitary of the Queen's Shiels, and, as an inscription above the door testifies, was built in 1868. The place was a favourite with the Prince Consort and it was because of his preference that Her Majesty erected the present building, which is never "lent" and is now rarely visited by the Court, though always ready for occupation. Between the Shiel and Dubh Loch a small cairn will be seen by the side of a bridle-path, close to a water-fall known as "The Stullan". It marks the spot where, on 3rd October, 1870, when the Queen was on a visit to Pannanich, the Marquis of Lorne proposed to the Princess Louise. Dubh Loch lies at an altitude of 2091 feet, at the base, on the South side, of the crags of Broad Cairn (3268 feet) and Cairn Bannoch (3314 feet), two summits on the county march with Forfar; on the North side it is confined by cliffs of Lochnagar. It is a tarn covering about sixty acres, and is described in "Leaves" as "very wild, the hills, which are very rocky and precipitous, rising perpendicularly from it". A wounded stag having here taken to the water, the Duke of Edinburgh, being the only swimmer of the party, followed it into the loch and gave the *coup de grace*.

'Tis a faëry spot—'tis a wild sweet glen,
And the Dee goes dancing by,
And the stars at even beyond our ken
On the hill-tops seem to lie.

Glen Gairn.

The River Gairn is the longest tributary of the Dee, and has a course of 20 miles, its principal head stream having its source on the summit of Ben Avon (3843 feet). For the first few miles of its course, it flows in the glen between Ben Avon on the North, and a lower range of hills, of which Culardoch (2953 feet) is the highest, on the South. Bending round the North side of Tom a' Chuir, a spur of Culardoch, it approaches within half a mile of Loch Builg, a Banffshire loch draining to the Avon. From this point the glen opens out, and, nearly three miles below, Corndavon Lodge is reached. The Gairn continues its Eastward course, past Rineaton, Rinloan, and Gairnshiel, till it receives Glenfinzie Burn, whence it flows South-east to the Dee, which it joins about a quarter of a mile below Bridge of Gairn. Cultivation is confined to a narrow belt, sometimes contracting to vanishing point, at others laboriously broadening into crofts. Sheep take the place of cattle where the heather-covered soil refuses to be tickled into crop-bearing; beyond the habitations of men the red deer claim sole possession.

Bridge of Gairn, a handsome, single-arched structure, is about a mile and a half from Ballater by the North road. A few yards above is a portion of its predecessor, which carried the old North road over the Gairn. The remains of the old parish church of Glengairn will be observed just below the bridge; the burial ground contains the grave of the last Mackenzie of Dalmore. On a little knoll about half a mile North-east from the bridge are the ruins of Gairn Castle, formerly a hunting seat of the Forbes family. Abergairn, on the left bank of the stream, a short distance above the bridge, has long been noted for its lead mines; but all attempts to work them have been commercially unsuccessful.

There is a road on each side of the Gairn, the chief one joining the North road a little to the West of the bridge. The road on the East side leads mainly to Morven Lodge and Glen Finzie. Taking the East road, a wool-mill, the corn-mill of Prony, and the reservoir of the Ballater Water-works will be passed. Above the bridge the Gairn is rather rocky at first, then rugged and stony. Two miles above Bridge of Gairn, Candacraig will be passed on the right, with, on the left bank of Lary Burn, a Roman Catholic Church. Crossing Lary Burn, the road, rapidly rising, leads on to Morven Lodge, a shooting-box on the Western slope of Morven. The easiest ascent of that mountain is made by driving to the Lodge, from which the summit is only about 2½ miles distant. Glenfinzie Burn joins the Gairn about half a mile above Lary Burn, and along Glen Finzie a road leads to Tornahaish on the Don.

Taking the road on the West side of the Bridge of Gairn, a direction-post there gives the following distances: Gairnshiel, 5 miles; Corndavon, 10½ miles; Loch Builg, 13¼ miles. Proceeding along this road and passing the mouth of Glen Finzie, on the opposite side of the river, Dalfad will be noticed, with an old burial-ground and the remains of a Roman Catholic chapel. Dalfad belonged to a branch of the persecuted Macgregors, and sent a considerable contingent to Culloden.

Gairnshiel is a shooting-box on the river-side. A "General Wade" bridge, built in 1750, in connection with the military road to Corgarff, here crosses the river; below this, on the left bank, is the *quoad sacra* church of Glengairn. Rinloan at one time boasted of an inn; Rineaton was long the property of Macdonalds who claimed descent from the Lords of the Isles, and their burial-aisle is close to the old mansion house.

Corndavon Lodge is a pleasantly situated shooting-box on the North side of the Gairn, on a slope of Brown Cow Hill (2721 feet). The only dwelling-house farther up the glen is Lochbuilg Cottage, occupied only during the shooting season. A road leading direct from Balmoral by Bridgend of Bush to Glen Gairn is preferred by drivers from Ballater to the glen road from Bridge of Gairn. An old drove road, the Bealach Dearg, crosses from the Dee *via* Invercauld to Loch Builg, and on to Inchrory and Tomintoul. The proprietor of Invercauld recently substituted a new road farther East, the better to avoid the deer forest. As Lochbuilg Cottage is neared the new road will be observed winding along Culardoch to the Gairn. Here the driving road terminates, but the mountaineer will find two paths leading towards the summit of Ben Avon.

THE BARON OF BRACKLEY.

1. Inverey cam doun Deeside, whistlin and playin,
He was at brave Braikley's yetts ere it was dawin.

2. 'He rappit fu loudly an wi a great roar,
Cried, Cum doun, cum doun, Braikley, and open the door.

3. 'Are ye sleepin, Baronne, or are ye wakin?
Ther's sharpe swords at your yett, will gar your blood spin.

4. 'Open the yett, Braikley, and lat us within,
Till we on the green turf gar your blood rin.'

5. Out spak the brave baronne, ower the castell-wa:
'Are ye come to spulzie and plunder mi ha?

6. 'But gin ye be gentlemen, licht an cum in:
Gin ye drink o my wine, ye'll nae gar my bluid spin.

7. 'Gin ye be hir'd widifus, ye may gang by,
Ye may gang to the lawlands and steal their fat ky.

8. 'Ther spulzie like rievers o wyld kettrin clan,
Who plunder unsparing baith houses and lan.

9. ‘Gin ye be gentlemen, licht an’ cum [in],
Ther’s meat an drink i my ha for every man.

10. ‘Gin ye be hir’d widifus, ye may gang by,
Gang doun to the lawlands, and steal horse and ky.’

11. Up spak his ladie, at his back where she lay,
‘Get up, get up, Braikley, and be not afraid;
The’r but young hir’d widifus wi belted plaids.’

12. ‘Cum kiss me, mi Peggy, I’ll nae langer stay,
For I will go out and meet Inverey.

13. ‘But haud your tongue, Peggy, and mak nae sic din.
For yon same hir’d widifus will prove themselves men.’

14. She called on her marys, they cam to her hand;
Cries, Bring me your rocks, lassies, we will them command.

15. ‘Get up, get up, Braikley, and turn back your ky,
Or me an mi women will them defy.

16. ‘Cum forth then, mi maidens, and show them some play;
We’ll ficht them, and shortly the cowards will fly.

17. ‘Gin I had a husband, whereas I hae nane,
He woud nae ly i his bed and see his ky taen.

18. ‘Ther’s four-and-twenty milk-whit calves, twal o them ky,
In the woods o Glentanner, its ther thei a’ ly.

19. ‘Ther’s goat i the Etnach, and sheep o the brae,
An a’ will be plundered by young Inverey.’

20. ‘Now haud your tongue, Peggy, and gie me a gun,
Ye’ll see me gae furth, but I’ll never cum in.

21. ‘Ca mi brother William, mi unkl also,
Mi cousin James Gordon; we’ll mount and we’ll go.’

22. When Braikley was ready and stood i the closs,
He was the bravest baronne that eer mounted horse.

23. Whan all wer assembled o the castell green,
No man like brave Braikley was ther to be seen.

24. . . . . . .
‘Turn back, brother William, ye are a bridegroom;

25. ‘ Wi bonnie Jean Gordon, the maid o the mill ;
O sichin and sobbin she'll soon get her fill.’

26. ‘ Im no coward, brother, 't is kend I'm a man :
I'll ficht i your quarral as lang's I can stand.

27. ‘ I'll ficht, my dear brother, wi heart and gude will,
And so will young Harry that lives at the mill.

28. ‘ But turn, mi dear brother, and nae langer stay :
What'll cum o your ladie, gin Braikley thei slay?

29. ‘ What'll cum o your ladie and bonnie young son?
O what'll cum o them when Braikley is gone?’

30. ‘ I never will turn: do you think I will fly?
But here I will ficht, and here I will die.’

31. ‘ Strik dogs,’ crys Inverey, ‘and ficht till ye're slayn,
For we are four hundred, ye are but four men.

32. ‘ Strik, strik, ye proud boaster, your honour is gone.
Your lands we will plunder, your castell we'll burn.’

33. At the head o the Etnach the battel began,
At Little Auchoilzie thei killed the first man.

34. First thei killed ane, and soon thei killed twa,
Thei killd gallant Braikley, the flour o them a'.

35. Thei killd William Gordon, and James o the Knox,
And brave Alexander, the flour o Glenmuick.

36. What sichin and moaning was heard i the glen,
For the Baronne o Braikley, who basely was slayn !

37. ‘ Cam ye bi the castell, and was ye in there?
Saw ye pretty Peggy tearing her hair?’

38. ‘ Yes, I cam by Braikley, and I gaed in there,
And there [saw] his ladie braiding her hair.

39. ‘ She was rantin, and dancin, and singin for joy,
And vowin that nicht she woud feest Inverey.

40. ‘ She ate wi him, drank wi him, welcomd him in,
Was kend to the man that had slain her baronne.’

41. Up spake the son on the nourice's knee,
' Gin I live to be a man, revenged I'll be.'

42. Ther's dool i the kitchin, and mirth i the ha,
The Baronne o Braikley is dead and awa.*

---

*From Child's "English and Scottish Popular Ballads," iv., p. 84, where it is reprinted from Laing's "Scarce Ancient Ballads," Aberdeen, 1822, and forms the "A" text of the various sets of the ballad there given. It is substantially the same as that given by Robertson in "The Deeside Guide," whose copy was built up two-thirds from the above, half-a-dozen stanzas from Jamieson's text, and half-a-dozen nearly or entirely from Dr. J. Hill Burton, or directly from some traditional source. The ballad was first printed by Jamieson in "Popular Ballads" (1806), i., p. 102.

Two or more different incidents, separated by a considerable lapse of time, have been mixed up in this ballad, notably the murder of the old Baron of Brackley in 1592, and the cattle raiding affray of September, 1666. It is quite possible that two separate ballads on these events have in the course of tradition got mixed into one. For a full detail of the whole circumstances see Child's Ballads, iv., p. 84.

XI.—BALLATER TO BALMORAL.

I.—By the South Road.

Here creeps among the nodding trees
The muted echo of a breeze,
Like humming of Hymettus' bees.

UNTIL the purchase of the estate of Balmoral by Prince Albert, there were public roads on both banks of the river all the way to Linn of Dee, but as the South road destroyed the amenity of the Castle and its policies, an arrangement was made in 1855 with the Road Trustees, whereby the public use of the portion between Balmoral Bridge and the old bridge at Invercauld was discontinued. Thus about seven miles of a beautiful old highway were closed; but on the whole the bargain was in favour of Deeside and the public.

The road from Ballater to Balmoral by the South side of the river is longer than and not so level as the one on the North side, and the view is frequently restricted by the proximity of the hills and the density of the forest. Yet it is exceedingly picturesque, and the favourite circular drive from Ballater is up the North and down the South side. In the description of Glen Muick we have included the South road as far as Knock Castle, which we pass on the right.

Here nature hangs her mantle green
On every budding tree,
And spreads her sheets o' daisies white
Out o'er the grassy lea.

Strath Girnock. After a considerable rise, the road descends towards the mouth of Strath Girnock. Two tree-clad hills, Creag Phiobaidh (1462 feet) on the East, and Creag Ghiubhais on the West, guard the mouth of the glen. The Girnock is crossed at a little hamlet with a Post-Office. The mansion house of Strath Girnock stood at the base of Creag Phiobaidh, but it has completely disappeared. The lairds, a branch of the Forbes family, were generally at feud with their neighbours of Knock. The last Forbes made an end of the matter, but only to the aggrandisement of his superior, the laird of Abergeldie. Forbes slew the seven sons of Knock as they were casting peats, sticking their heads on "flauchter" spades; and on hearing the terrible news the old man fell down dead. Thereupon Gordon of Abergèldie came on the scene; Forbes was hanged on his own roof-tree, his lands being forfeited to the judge, who also acquired, at the same time, the estate of Knock in succession to his kinsman. There are a few farms, but the population in the Strath, as in other Highland glens, has considerably decreased. Formerly it was particularly noted for smuggling, no fewer than a dozen "black bothies" being at one time in operation in the upper part of the little glen. The road leading from the Dee at Balmoral to Glen Muick at Inschnabobart crosses the Girnock about a mile and a half below its source. The Coyles of Muick slope to the Girnock on the West.

Creag nam Ban (1730 feet) is another finely-wooded hill, descending abruptly to the Dee West of Creag Ghiubhais. The Queen writes that the finding of a piece of white heather on Creag nam Ban by the Crown Prince of Prussia gave him an opportunity of making "an allusion to his hopes and wishes" to the Princess Royal. According to tradition the name of the hill, "the women's crag", is due to the fact that of old witches were burned on the summit; the hollow where the stake was fixed is still pointed out. Three hundred years ago the laird of Abergeldie had judicially devolved on him the trial of a certain witch—this is matter of history; legend adds that a well-known witch, Katie Rankie, was removed from the castle dungeon to suffer on Creag nam Ban. Passing Corby Hall, the royal vegetable garden, Abergeldie will be reached.

Bonnie lassie, will ye go,
To the Birks o' Abergeldie?

Abergeldie Castle.

Abergeldie has been leased in connection with Balmoral since Her Majesty came to reside on Deeside, its possession being essential to the amenities of the Royal residence. It belongs to Mr. Hugh Mackay Gordon, and was anciently the property of the Mowats. There is a tradition concerning one of the Mowats that he exercised his powers so ruthlessly that "his 'Tree' was hardly ever teeme". Early in the 16th century, Sir Alexander Gordon of Midmar, second son of the first Earl of Huntly, received a charter of the lands, and from him they have descended to the present proprietor, the sixteenth Gordon in possession. The estate lies contiguous to that of Balmoral, and the Castle is retained by the Queen for distinguished visitors. Among the royal residents may be named the late Duchess of Kent, the Prince of Wales, and the Empress Eugenie. "The Castle has been much altered and added to, but it still retains the original tower which formed the nucleus of the whole, and which, with its rounded angles, its crow-stepped gables and its somewhat elaborately corbelled angle turret, is a good and picturesque example of the 16th century manor house in Aberdeenshire". The "dungeon" below the old staircase is still extant, as is also the ring to

Abergeldie Castle.

which prisoners were bound. At the Revolution and after the Rebellion of 1715 it was garrisoned by Government troops. It faces the South road, the main entrance door being "adorned" with a horse shoe "for luck". An uninscribed standing-stone, some six feet in height, fronts the castle. The Dee at one time flowed on the South side of the Castle, the old channel extending from Drymill, below the suspension bridge near Easter Balmoral, to Corby Hall. The birch wine formerly made at Abergeldie had quite a reputation, as well as the birches themselves, one writer calls it "delicious", another, "superior to the finest champagne". The last occasion on which there is record of its use at the Castle was at the funeral of the laird who died in 1831; but so late as 1845 it was sold at Birkhall at the modest price of a shilling per bottle.

Communication between the Castle and the North side of the river was formerly maintained by means of a "cradle" running on a rope suspended from upright posts on each side of the Dee. In 1885, a handsome suspension foot-bridge was erected by the Queen.

Geldie Burn joins the Dee about 200 yards West of Abergeldie Castle. About half a mile up this burn, in a field still known as Chapel Park, is the site of St. Columba's Chapel, with a small burial ground, fringed with trees. A short distance to the South is the little hamlet of Khantore.

Clachanturn is about three quarters of a mile beyond Abergeldie Castle. Formerly a large market was held here, and some almanacks publish that it is still held. Almost the only part left of the once populous clachan is a "smiddy". It was formerly a complaint in highland parishes that "since the disuse of arms, there is scarcely a tolerable smith to be met with".

There is a suspension bridge for foot passengers over the Dee about three quarters of a mile West from Clachanturn. A short distance up the brae, to the South, is the Lochnagar Distillery. The old South road entered the Balmoral grounds at Easter Balmoral, a neat village a little West of the suspension bridge. Passing it on the left, the South road soon terminates at the Bridge Lodge of Balmoral Castle, where it crosses the Dee by a handsome bridge, erected by the late Prince Consort, and joins the North road. Between the two bridges, several statues in the Castle grounds will be passed, as well as a neat drinking fountain by the roadside, erected by the Queen in remembrance of Sir Thomas Biddulph, for many years Keeper of the Privy Purse, who died at Mains of Abergeldie in 1878.

II.—By the North Road.

> Yet often thy thoughts may in after years roam
> To the scene of thy life's morn—thy loved Highland home ;
> And true shall our hearts beat to thee and to thine,
> While the Dee runs its course or Craig Nich rears a pine.

The road between Ballater and Braemar, Balmoral Castle being about equi-distant from both places, is generally considered the finest in Aberdeenshire. During the summer and autumn months it is more frequented than any other similar stretch of road (16½ miles) in the county. Westward from Ballater the valley of the Dee lends itself less and less to cultivation, for the strath narrows, the mountains pressing upon the banks of the river. The scenery becomes wilder, yet always picturesque, never monotonous. The lower hills, often with bold rocky fronts, are generally tree-clad with Scottish fir, larch and birch, while, for most of the way, Lochnagar, with its irregular contour and magnificent corries, compels admiration. Rounding the base of Craigendarroch and crossing Bridge of Gairn, the traveller will find himself, half a mile West of the latter point, opposite a neat suspension bridge

(Polhollick) over the Dee, the gift of the late Mr. Alexander Gordon. A few yards short of the 45th mile-stone, on the opposite side of the river, will be observed the mouth of the Girnock with its guardian hills and islets. Two of the latter are wooded, but the third, which dates only from 1881, is tree-less. Half a mile further Westward, 3½ miles from Ballater, is the old-established hostel of Coillecriech. Looking backwards there is a capital view of Craigendarroch, with the deep gully of the Pass of Ballater. South of the Dee rise the green-topped Coyles of Muick, while to the West there seems to be an amphitheatre of hills, all more or less rocky and covered with heather, pine, and birch.

A little below the 47th mile-stone, on the right hand side of the road, may still be seen traces of the site of the chapel of Micras, readily recognised by a "Standing Stone", which is believed to have formed part of a Druidical circle, but was latterly used as a reading desk. The chapel stood at the base of Geallaig (2439 feet), the most prominent hill close to the North side of the road between Ballater and Balmoral. This hill would be monotonous for its length were it not for the occasional breaks in the outline, trees, especially birches, frequently bristling to the summit. Wester Micras is just beyond the 48th mile-stone, almost opposite Abergeldie Castle. The hamlet was a rather straggling one, and, till recently, of a poor type; now, however, it shews considerable improvement. Between Torgalter, a farm on the brae immediately opposite Abergeldie Castle, and Wester Micras, was another chapel, near a mountain ash which may be seen from the road.

Passing Abergeldie Castle and the Free Church of Crathie, a road will be observed, about a quarter of a mile West from the 49th mile-stone, leading to the suspension bridge over the Dee near Easter Balmoral. A few yards beyond this road, at the base of Craig Ghuie, and on the North side of the main road, is the Established Church, the foundation-stone of which was laid on September 11th, 1893, by Her Majesty the Queen, who was also present at the opening on June 18th, 1895. On the opposite side is the manse, with an old, ruined, ivy-clad church and the churchyard. This church was a pre-Reformation building, and was in use till 1804. It was dedicated to St. Miniar—a name surviving in a neighbouring pool of the river—and held of the Abbey of Cambuskenneth. One is struck with the number of tombstones bearing names in Gaelic, a language which, though now rapidly disappearing in upper Deeside, was used in Crathie church till 1830. Not a few servants of the Royal Household who died at Balmoral are buried here, and to each an appropriate headstone has been erected by Her Majesty. The most interesting of these is that placed over the grave of John Brown, the Queen's personal attendant. Brown's family belonged to the parish, for generations; the saying that a prophet has no honour in his own country is inapplicable in this instance. The site of the present handsome church was occupied by an exceedingly plain structure, quite "barn-like" in appearance, where the Queen regularly worshipped when at Balmoral. The new church, which is seated for about 450, is built of Inver granite in the form of a cross, with a square tower at the East end rising above the construction of the nave and transepts. The main entrance is at the West gable, and is marked by a beautiful open porch in ornamental woodwork. The Queen's transept on the South side of the building is approached by a magnificent little porch, surmounted by the memorial window erected by Her Majesty, and on the North side immediately opposite, is the heritors' transept and vestry. The

Crathie Church.

East end is in the form of an apse, lighted with lancet windows. The tower, which is of the same material as the walls, is the most striking feature of the structure. It rises to a total height of 95 feet, or 45 feet above the ridge of the roof of the church. The belfry has been provided with four bells, presented by Princesses Louise and Beatrice. They are mechanically fitted, and are played by a key board, which occupies a room above the apse of the church. The entire cost of the church was about £6000, of which £2400 was raised by a bazaar. The interior, especially the woodwork, presents a particularly pleasing and chaste appearance. The seats and other decorative parts of the apse are of oak, richly moulded and carved. The Queen's seat is in the centre of the front row of stalls in the South transept. In front it is divided into five beautifully carved panels, spaced off with hand-wrought pinnacles. Immediately behind the Queen's seat are the Royal Arms boldly carved in oak. The whole of the seats in the Queen's transept are upholstered in purple velvet, and in the North transept the ends of the stalls are surmounted by finials in the form of crowns. Richly carved oak screens have been placed behind both transepts. Seats have been placed for the elders round the circle of the apse, and immediately above these, the oak, reaching up to the dressed stone work, is beautifully wrought into panels.

The parishes of Crathie and Braemar were, at some unknown time, united; now, *quoad sacra*, they have been disjoined. The civil parish of Crathie-Braemar is one of the largest in Scotland, extending to the head-streams of the Dee and the Western boundary of Aberdeenshire, a length of 28 miles.

Nearly half a mile beyond the church, Crathie Burn joins the Dee. Another mark of the old North road may be observed here—the remains of the old bridge over the burn, several yards above the new one. A direction-post here, on a side road, gives the following distances: Gairnshiel, 5 miles; Corndavon, 5¾ miles; Loch Builg, 8 ¼ miles.

On to the gentle Lady's halls
Who wears old Scotland's crown.

Balmoral Castle.

Balmoral Castle stands at an altitude of 926 feet above sea level on the South side of the Dee, opposite the 50th mile-stone, on a terraced haugh close to the river, with magnificent natural surroundings. The castle is embosomed among pines and birches, while pines rise above it on the slope of Lochnagar, and the ornamental grounds are splendidly laid out and planted with trees and shrubs of many varieties. The building, site, and surroundings are alike grand; and no one who has seen them will wonder why Her Majesty spends a considerable portion of each year on Deeside: "every year my heart becomes more fixed in this dear Paradise" ("Leaves"). The castle is in the Scottish Baronial style of architecture, but with several deviations and innovations tending to assure the greater comfort and accommodation of the residents. Thus the building combines the characteristics of an ancient stronghold with those of a modern residence. Prince Albert (it is understood) designed its main features, and the plans were supplied by the late Mr. William Smith, City Architect of Aberdeen. The castle consists of two blocks connected by wings, with a tower rising to the height of one hundred feet at the Eastern extremity. It has an unusually elegant and bright appearance, having been built of finely-dressed granite of a light grey colour, obtained within a short distance. The stone is treated with a severe yet elegant simplicity and chasteness of design, as well as with exquisiteness of workmanship. Many additions have been made to the original building, the whole now affording accommodation for about 120 persons. The internal furnishings are plain, but in the finest taste.

The estate of Balmoral at one time formed part of the princely possessions of the Earldom of Mar. In the beginning of the 17th century, the Earl of Mar granted the estate to John Farquharson, second son of the first Farquharson of Inverey. The last Farquharson of Balmoral, known as the "Baron Ban", died without issue subsequent to 1746, when the estate fell to the Farquharsons of Auchendryne and Inverey, who in the end of the last century sold it, along with Auchendryne and Inverey, to the Earl of Fife. The Earl's trustees leased the property to the Right Hon. Sir Robert Gordon, brother of the (Premier) Earl of Aberdeen, in the second quarter of the present century. Sir Robert Gordon added considerably to the small "house" which he found on the estate, and the "old castle" had latterly a somewhat imposing appearance. When Sir Robert died in 1847, Prince Albert acquired the reversion of his lease, and accordingly, on 8th September, 1848, Her Majesty first arrived at Balmoral, after having landed at Aberdeen. Some years afterwards Prince Albert bought the estate, which stretches to the summit of Lochnagar, and a cairn on Craig Gowan was erected to "commemorate the purchase of the Balmoral Estate, October 11th, 1852". As the old castle proved quite inadequate for royal requirements, the erection of a new structure was resolved upon, and the present building was completed in August, 1856. The estate is now the property of the Queen, and

Her Majesty has increased its extent on the West by purchasing Ballochbuie Forest from Invercauld. The rising ground to the South of the castle is dotted with the residences of the Royal servants.

Reference has already been made to several memorials erected by the Queen, and numerous others could be mentioned. Prince Albert's cairn, of pyramidal form, is, from many points, a commanding erection. It tops Creag an Lurachain (1437 feet), one of the summits of Creag a' Ghobhainn, better known as Craig Gowan, which rises immediately to the South of Balmoral Castle. Craig Gowan, a beautiful hill covered with birches, is of almost historical importance; numerous bonfires have here commemorated royal and national events, including celebrations of the fall of Sevastopol and the surrender of Pretoria. A bronze statue of the Prince, by Theed, and an obelisk raised to his memory by the Royal tenantry, as well as a bronze statue of the Queen, erected by the Royal tenantry and the servants of the Household, stand within the castle grounds. But there are numerous monuments within the policies; and "cairns", named after members of the Royal Family, surmount several of the hills upon the estate.

XII.—BALMORAL TO BRAEMAR.

Gladly we breathe the breeze that blew from lofty Lochnagar,
And our eyes roam freely o'er the purple braes of broad Braemar.

LEAVING the Royal Palace behind, in a few yards a road leading Northwards will be observed on the right. It is a branch of the road already mentioned as leading to Loch Builg, and no visitor should pass without going a short distance up the brae, where he will obtain the finest view of Balmoral Castle and Lochnagar—one of the loveliest prospects on Deeside.

Hark ! hark ! it is the horn
On mountain breezes borne.
Awake ! it is the morn :
Awake, Monaltrie !

Monaltrie.

The original House of Monaltrie stood on rising ground to the right, a little short of the 51st mile-stone. The name is still retained in "Mains of Monaltrie", about half a mile from the road. The old house was burned while occupied by Government troops after the battle of Culloden. At one time a double row of houses known as the "Street of Monaltrie" here lined the road, having been erected for old Highland soldiers on their return from the American War of Independence.

Carn na Cuimhne. Carn na Cuimhne (the Cairn of Remembrance) corrupted to Cairnaquheen will next interest the tourist. It is a few yards beyond the 51st. mile-stone, on the South side of the road, close to the bank of the river, and is surmounted by a flag-staff and vane, and enclosed by a low stone dyke, within which are a few trees. "Carn na Cuimhne" is the "slogan" of the Farquharsons. The tradition is that every clansman mustered for battle placed a stone on it, and in returning each survivor removed a stone, the number left thus representing those who had been slain.

Now to the mountain's peak,
Whence hills in glory spread,
Hasten, O Nature's child.

Glen Gelder. Opposite Carn na Cuimhne is the mouth of the Gelder, a burn which, issuing from the Loch of Lochnagar, enters the Dee between Craig Gowan and Canup Hill (1477 feet), the latter surmounted by the Princess Royal's Cairn. Glen Gelder may, at certain seasons, be advantageously used as a direct route to Lochnagar. The glen lies within the Balmoral grounds, and contains the lonely Gelder Shiel erected by the Queen: "it contains only two small rooms and a little kitchen. It stands in a very wild, solitary spot, looking up to Lochnagar, which towers up immediately above the house". Several *larachs* testify that at one time the glen was partly under cultivation; now the only arable land is at Invergelder, the home farm of Balmoral, near the mouth of the burn. The Woods of Garmaddie stretch Westward from Invergelder along the South bank of the Dee.

Inver.

The Fearder Burn enters the Dee on the left bank about half a mile above the Gelder, Creag an Orduigh (1598 feet), locally corrupted to Craig Nortie, commanding the left bank between it and the burn at Monaltrie. The burn crossed, we practically leave birches behind, and enter a pine-clad region. Mill of Inver stands at the point where the road crosses the Fearder, and a quarter of a mile beyond, near the 52nd mile-stone, is the Invercauld Arms, better known as Inver Inn, a few yards West of which we get a peep of the rocky summits of Ben Avon. Behind the Inn is Creag na Spaine (1542 feet), a picturesquely tree-clad rock. Ben Avon and Beinn a' Bhuird may be visited from here; while, on the opposite side of the Dee, Lochnagar is within convenient distance. The old Inn was on the other (South) side of the road; on 9th September, 1715, the Earl of Mar wrote from Braemar directing the Kildrummy men to assemble there "on the following Monday".

There mountains vie with purple heath,
With many a gloomy vale beneath,
While down the rocks the torrents flow
To some dark corrie far below.

Aberarder.

Aberarder, as the district comprised within the valley of the Fearder Burn is known, was once very populous, and had a chapel, burial ground, and (bonnet) lairds of its own. There are still several farms and crofts in the glen, but its elevation of over 1000 feet above sea level is by no means favourable to cultivation. Fearder Burn rises between Culardoch and Carn Liath (2821 feet), the Bealach Dearg crossing between them at a height of about 2250 feet. The farthest up farm in the glen was Auchnagymlinn, but in the flood of 1829 it was destroyed by sand and gravel. In the forkings of the burn, above Auchnagymlinn, may be seen the grave of a "giant", the last of his race, 'tis said, which is satisfactory, as the "grave" is about 20 feet long. Auchtavan is now the highest farm, a name said to mean "the field of two kids", two kids being probably the original rent. St. Manire Chapel, of which there are still slight indications, stood at Balmore, below Auchtavan; the burial ground is overshadowed by a stunted larch tree. Near this chapel there was held a market, which in later times was removed to a stance near the manse of Crathie, and thence to Clachanturn. Balnoe lies to the South of Balmore, and a little to the West the new road, designed to supersede the Bealach Dearg, breaks off from the glen road towards Loch Builg. (Distances from Braemar: Loch Builg, 13 miles; Inchrory, 16 miles; Tomintoul, 24 miles; Ballindalloch, 40 miles.) Still lower is Ballachlaggan, where a Baillie of Strathdee is said to have summarily tried and hanged no fewer than eighteen "bonnet" lairds. On the left bank of the Fearder, about half a mile North from Inver Inn, the Farm of Tullochcoy will be observed. The mansion house of Tullochcoy was built in 1693 by John Farquharson of the Monaltrie branch of the family; a stone still bears the inscription: "I.F: A.O. 1693". The house was partly rebuilt in the beginning of the present century. Tullochcoy was "out in the '15", and had to part with his patrimony to his relation the laird of Invercauld, thereupon removing to Balnaboddach in Glen Bucket, where a descendant still resides.

> I've stretched me 'mang the forest trees
> On shaggy Ballochbuie;
> I've traced the "infant rills" o' Dee
> By towerin' Ben Muich Dhui.

Ballochbuie Forest.

Resuming the journey to Braemar, the pine and birch bordered road runs for about two miles from Inver Inn through a flat narrow strip known as the Muir of Inver. Some might call the Muir monotonous, especially at a part where the almost houseless road is uncompromisingly unbending. But the mixture of fir and larch never seems to pall; the lighter green of the larches brightens the scene. Anon the Dee will be seen "glintin" through the trees as it flows merrily along. Indeed, the sound of the hurrying river is a sonata; now heard as though it were the wind playing among the pines; then there's a brattling and a clattering, followed by a hum like the distant sound of a great crowd, toned and subdued into a pleasant ever-changing melody. Meall Alvie (1841 feet) dominates the North side of the river about 1½ miles South-west from Creag na Spaine; on the opposite side of the Dee is the famed Ballochbuie Forest, which, according to tradition, was sold to Farquharson of Invercauld for a tartan plaid by McGregor, the last laird of Ballochbuie. In allusion to this circumstance the Queen has erected a stone with the following inscription: "Queen Victoria entered into possession of Ballochbuie on the 15th day of May, 1878. 'The bonniest plaid in Scotland'". A little short of the 55th mile-stone a private bridge crosses the Dee, giving access, from the North, to Danzig Shiel, a small royal cottage in the heart of the Ballochbuie Forest. A few yards above this bridge the Garbh Allt, whose head streams rise on Lochnagar, joins the Dee after running through the Forest.

> Here, oft by wild and wimpling stream,
> From alpine summits bald,
> The bard has sung his doric theme—
> "The Bowers of Invercauld".

About three quarters of a mile above Danzig Bridge the river is crossed by a romantic-looking old bridge known as Bridge of Dee, erected by General Wade in connection with the military road from Blairgowrie, by Corgarff and Grantown, to Inverness. Like many of the General's bridges it is high in the centre. It was built of stones obtained from Craig Clunie, on the South side of the Dee, in the immediate vicinity, no tool marks being visible on many of them. By the arrangement made for shutting-up part of the South road, the bridge is now the property of the Queen, but the public are allowed to use it in visiting the Falls of Garbh Allt. The Falls, while not remarkable for volume of water, are beautiful cascades much frequented by tourists. They are three in number, the lowermost, which is the largest, plunging into a big dark pool. Here the burn is crossed by an iron foot-bridge. It is said there is an ancient right-of-way by the Falls, up the burn and along the "Smuggler's Shank", to Glen Doll and Glen Clova in Forfarshire. The "Shank" was so named from having been much used by smugglers to convey whiskey on horseback from Deeside to the South, and the route is still occasionally traversed by mountaineers in Her Majesty's absence from Balmoral.

Old Bridge of Dee, Invercauld.

Invercauld Bridge, erected at the expense of Prince Albert on the closing of the Ballochbuie road, is about 150 yards above General Wade's bridge. It is a handsome granite structure, and commands a fine view, the Dee being here diversified by miniature rapids over a channel of slaty quartzose rock. We have always found it impossible to cross the river here without a long look up the Dee and a long look down. Up—a fir- and birch-clad crag closes the view, while the broadened channel has turned bouldery; down—birches and pines fringe the South bank, and the graceful Stuc Eoin of Lochnagar bounds the prospect, while the foreground is occupied by the grey old bridge, with miniature trees growing among its arches. Duncan Calder, the seer of Glen Lui, prophesied that a thorn bush would grow from a pool here—and was laughed at. But in 1752 the pool was spanned by Wade's bridge, and in course of time a thorn bush shewed itself on one of the piers. At the West end of the bridge a small burn, Allt na Claise Moire (the burn of the big hollow), enters the Dee. There is a "short cut" along this burn to Auchallater, a sheep-grazing farm, at the mouth of Glen Callater. A little beyond is the Western entrance to Ballochbuie Forest.

> 'Mid rocky, wooded, rugged hills,
> And music from the countless rills
> That rush adown their frowning sides,
> Proud Invercauld in state presides.

Invercauld. Invercauld House, on the North side of the river, is approached from the East by a road branching off the North road opposite Bridge of Dee, and there is also a right-of-way Westward along the

North bank of the river. In several places, however, particularly between Invercauld House and the Quoich, this public road has been allowed to become somewhat impracticable for carriages. A stone below Invercauld House near the left bank of the Dee gives the height, about 6½ feet above the level of the haugh, of the river on 4th August, 1829, at 8 a.m. East of Invercauld there is a road, by Keiloch, Felagie, and Aberarder, on the *North* side of Meall Alvie and Creag na Spaine, to the North road near Mill of Inver.

The Farquharsons of Invercauld are the only survivors, by the female line, of the old families of Braemar; history allows them a genealogy of centuries, but tradition, as usual, goes beyond fact. One story has it that the founder acquired his position by a clever ruse: snow was rapidly melting in the corries of Beinn a' Bhuird when a wily shepherd approached the house and asked leave for his sheep to pasture on the haugh till the snow should disappear. The desired permission was granted, and the shepherd and his flock became permanent residents, on the ground that snow was always to be found on Beinn a' Bhuird! The present writer may not be considered quite impartial on the beauty of Deeside scenery; read therefore what Maculloch says: "At Invercauld the views are exceedingly fine. Among many that might be named, those in which Lochnagar, on one hand, and Beinn a' Bhuird, on the other, form the extreme distances, are perhaps the most striking. Finer mountain outlines cannot be imagined than those in which the former hill is implicated: so graceful is its pyramidal shape, and so beautifully contrasted and varied are all the lines and forms of the mountains

CHEM

Invercauld House.

out of which it rises, king of all; while they seem to cluster round it as the monarch of all the surrounding country. . . . The character of the scenery is much changed where Beinn a' Bhuird bounds the distance; nor can we help admiring how nature contrives to produce grandeur from forms the most opposite". The chieftain of the Farquharson clan, John Farquharson, was an unwilling leader in the rising of 1715, for the Earl of Mar involved him in the action of the Jacobites by assigning him a post of honour in their army. The principal adherents of the old dynasty met in Invercauld House to arrange their plans, and from that mansion, for nearly the last time in Scotland, the "fiery cross" was sent forth over hill and glen. In 1745 the Invercauld chieftain was still alive, but took no part in the rebellion, although most of the Farquharsons "went out" under the laird of Monaltrie. The mansion house is a princely building, both externally and internally, and for situation is unrivalled on Deeside. In 1875 it was greatly enlarged—indeed practically reconstructed—but the old historic dining-hall is still almost the same as in the time of the Stuarts. The architectural style is Scottish Baronial, the principal feature being a battlemented tower, rising to the height of about 70 feet. The view from the house is superb. The Dee, winding through a narrow valley carpeted with green, can be followed for miles. To the South rise pine- and birch-clad rocks and crags, discernible amongst them being the mist over the Falls of Garbh Allt, while above towers Lochnagar with its storm-scarred peaks. On the North-west Beinn a' Bhuird rears its massive form, its corrie'd sides shewing great gashes and fissures, the results of long-continued elemental wars. Between Invercauld and the Linn of Dee there is about eight miles of the finest glen scenery in the Highlands; in the month of August, with the heather in full bloom, the beauty and richness of colouring are past description.

Returning to Invercauld Bridge, and pursuing the road to Braemar, a big stone will soon be observed on the right, the "Meikle Stane o' Clunie", which seems to have fallen from Craig Clunie, on the opposite side of the road. It is stated to have formed one of the landmarks between the properties of the Erskines or McGregors of Ballochbuie and the Farquharsons of Invercauld, and to have also been a haunt of the fairies. A few yards beyond the 56th mile-stone is the "Charter Chest", a recess in the rocky precipitous face of Craig Clunie, about 200 yards above the road, capable of admitting two men, but naturally rather difficult of access. Here the Invercauld titles and papers were concealed in the troublous times after the '15. Tradition also asserts that the laird himself hid there, and had frequently the mortification of hearing the government troops making merry at Invercauld. About a quarter of a mile short of the 57th mile-stone is another noted tree-clad crag—the Lion's Face, composed of slaty quartzose rock. The rocks on the upper part of the crag were fancifully believed at one time to have a lion-like contour, which the growth of the trees has quite hidden. In the beginning of the present century the crag was known as the Lion's Head. The valley of the Dee between Invercauld Bridge and Castletown is ruggedly picturesque as one looks up to these bristling crags, almost pastoral when the eye rests on the long haugh of Invercauld. A road leads direct from the Lion's Face by Dubh Chlais (black hollow), on the South side of Creag Choinnich, to the village of Braemar. This right-of-way, known as the "Lion's Face Road", is, by an arrangement between the proprietor and the Scottish Rights of Way and Recreation Society (Limited), shut against the public from 20th September to 30th November each year. The turnpike now rounds Creag Choinnich (Kenneth's Crag), a rocky height attaining an altitude of 1764 feet, in the East angle of the Dee and the Clunie Water, surmounted by a cairn erected by men of the 25th Regiment when stationed at Braemar Castle. Half a mile short of the village of Braemar the castle and churchyard will be passed on the right, the latter at the 58th mile-stone—the last of the series from Aberdeen.

The estates and proprietors in the parish of Crathie-Braemar are: Balmoral, Her Majesty the Queen; Abergeldie, Hugh M. Gordon; Invercauld, Alexander H. Farquharson; and Mar, the Duke of Fife, K.T.

XIII.—BRAEMAR.

The Standard's on the Braes o' Mar,
Its ribbons streaming rarely;
The gathering pipes on Lochnagar
Are sounding lang and sairly.

THE term "Braemar" has two applications—one to the district generally, or the old parish of Braemar; the other to the village, which may be regarded as its centre. The village is of great antiquity, and was of old known as Kyndrochet (Bridge-end), a name still met with in the district. Situated on both banks of the Clunie Water, about half a mile above its confluence with the Dee, the name Auchendryne is applied to the portion on the left bank, and Castletown to that on the right bank; though the name Castletown of Braemar is often applied to the whole village. "Castletown" is derived from Malcolm Canmore having had a castle, the ruins of which are still to be seen, at the East end of the bridge over the Clunie. It has long been known as Kyndrochet Castle; the ruins—which are not seen to advantage—indicate that it must have been a building of considerable size. Practically only the vaults, or dungeons, remain, for the materials of the walls have been utilised in the usual manner. There is a tradition—for which, however, we know of no grounds—that the castle was finally destroyed by artillery planted at Tomintoul on Morrone. Recently while workmen were removing what appeared to be a heap of rubbish at a point that seemed to be outside the castle enclosure, they discovered that they were working on a part of the massive castle wall, probably a portion of the South-western tower. The uncovered wall was found to be 11 feet thick, and on the inner side a stone staircase leading to the lower chambers was unearthed. The steps are of freestone, and measure 3 feet 3 inches in length, and are of light colour. The chisel marks are yet as distinct as when the steps came from the dresser. It is a spiral stair, and the outer ends of the steps are as nicely circled as if moulded out of wood. It is supposed, from the quality of the freestone, that it had been taken from Kildrummy. Robert II. granted several charters while here. Kenneth II. also had a hunting seat here, and Creag Choinnich refers to him, for, according to tradition, he watched the chase from it. While Ballater is indisputably the commercial capital of upper Deeside, Braemar is the fashionable one. Against the youth of Ballater as a place of importance we may set the fact that Braemar, with its ancient intimate associations with Royalty and the Court, fell from being a royal residence till, in the beginning of the present century, it was one of the meanest of Highland clachans. It then consisted of a number of low, smoky, thatched, straggling buildings, overgrown with grass and noisome weeds. There was but one inn, "more suitable for drovers and excise officers than any higher description of travellers". But that condition of matters has passed away, for, as Deeside came into general notice, Braemar gradually acquired the premier position as a health resort. Its isolation, however, coupled with building restrictions, has prevented its attaining the popularity of Ballater; and, being a more expensive place, its summer and autumn residents are of a more select class. The course of time has again brought Royalty to Deeside, and thus increased the attractions of Braemar. The number of visitors during "the season" is estimated at 10,000. Situated 1110 feet above the sea level, it has the most bracing climate on Deeside, and the surrounding scenery is fully as diversified and attractive as any of the resorts that have made Deeside famous. The churchyard, with the site of the old chapel of St. Andrew, might appear to indicate that the "Kirktown" had at one time been in its immediate neighbourhood. But the centre of population had always been near Kyndrochet Castle, which indeed at one period gave its name to the parish. About 1230 the church was given by Duncan, Earl of Mar, to the Priory of St. Mary of Monymusk. On the site of the chapel in the churchyard now stands the burial vault of the Farquharsons of Invercauld. The Mackenzies of Dalmore, the predecessors of the Duke of Fife, had burial ground close to its West end, as well as in the churchyard of Glengairn. One of the tombstones marks the last resting-place of the oldest, and probably latest surviving, "rebel" in Scotland, "Peter Grant, sometime Farmer in Dubrach, who died at Auchendryne, the 11th of Feb., 1824, aged 110 years". He was generally called "Dubrach" from the name of his farm (Dubh-bhruach), and the attention of George IV. having been directed to him he received a pension. Another interesting tombstone, erected to the memory of James Gruar, who died in 1807, states that the Gruars had burial ground there for 450 years. A head-stone of light granite affords an example of Her Majesty's appreciation of faithful service, and her well-known kindness as a mistress. On the West side of the churchyard a road leads to the river, where there was a ferry in connection with the Bealach Dearg.

A few yards to the North-east of the churchyard is Braemar Castle, which may be accounted the

Braemar Castle.

legitimate successor of Kyndrochet. In 1715 the Mar estates were forfeited on the attainder of the Earl, and were afterwards purchased by Lords Dun and Grange, from whom, in 1730, Farquharson of Invercauld acquired the castle and its lands. In 1748, he leased the remains of the castle to the War Office, with 14 acres of ground, for 99 years, at the yearly rent of £14. The Government then built the present castle, which served for many years as barracks for soldiers to keep the Highlanders in check. A guard of honour was stationed here during Her Majesty's earlier visits to Balmoral. For about half a century past a more peaceful "gathering of the clans" than that of the '15 or '45 has been held at the castle, almost every year, under the auspices of the Braemar Royal Highland Society. A race up Creag Choinnich was formerly one of the items in the programme, but was discontinued at the Queen's desire on account of the competitors over-exerting themselves. Malcolm Canmore is credited with the institution of this race, rewarding with a purse of gold, and a full set of dress and arms, the competitor who first reached the top! The interior of the castle has recently been modernised, and it is now let.

Upon the opposite side of the Dee will be observed, on a little knoll, a granite obelisk erected, "by his tenantry and servants, to whom he was greatly attached", to the memory of James Farquharson of Invercauld, who died in 1862; and close to it the Sluggan Burn enters the Dee. Along Glen Sluggan there is a path leading to the Quoich, and on to Beinn a' Bhuird and Ben Avon; there is a small shooting-box near the head of the glen. Here a stone of the house in which Findla Mohr was born is shewn; he was the common ancestor of the Farquharsons, including those of Inverey, Auchendryne and Castletown, Tullochcoy, Monaltrie, Balmoral, Finzean and Whitehouse. The Queen ascended Beinn a' Bhuird on 6th September, 1850, and "came upon a number of 'Cairngorms', which we all began picking up, and found some very pretty ones". A Cairngorm stone from Ben Avon, weighing about fifty pounds, is preserved in Invercauld House.

The first building passed, as Castletown is entered from the East, is the Invercauld Arms Hotel. On a mound here, on 6th September, 1715, previous to the Southward march by Spital of Glen Shee, John Erskine, 39th Earl of Mar, amid a great gathering of clansmen, planted the standard of the Chevalier de St. George, whom he had previously at Glenlivat proclaimed King, by the title of James VIII. This historic mound was covered in 1860 by an extension of the hotel buildings, and a plate, thus inscribed, records the fact: "On this spot the Earl of Mar raised his Standard of Rebellion. 1715". The Standard was elaborately wrought by the Countess of Mar, but an evil omen happened at its unfurling—the golden ball on the top fell, and the accident had a depressing effect on the assembled Highlanders, some of whom had been compelled against their own wish to join in the Rising.

The bridge on the Clunie connecting the two portions of the village, as well as the estates of Invercauld on the East, and Mar on the West, is a well-known structure, spanning the stream where it rushes along in a narrow, rocky gorge of quartzose mica-slate. The granite tors of Ben Avon form the background as one looks over the North parapet of the bridge; and on the South will be seen the "Mill on the Clunie", which has received an extraordinary amount of attention from artists and photographers. The Post Office, Roman Catholic Chapel, and Free Church are in Auchendryne; the Established and Episcopal Churches are in Castletown; while there is a "Jubilee Hall" in Auchendryne and another in Castletown, so jealous is each division of its individuality. *The Statistical Account* (1795) states that a branch of the Post Office was "lately" extended from Aberdeen to Kincardine O'Neil, 32 miles distant. This was doubtless considered "a great boon", as the inhabitants of Braemar had formerly to send a man weekly to Coupar-Angus for letters.

As Creag Choinnich commands the Eastern angle formed by the Clunie with the Dee, so Mor Shron (2819 feet) dominates Braemar from the Western angle. The name, which signifies the big nose, has been corrupted into Morrone. The summit is a little over two miles from the village, and will be found, by those making the ascent, to be rather deceptively situated. The nearer views, as the ascent is made, well repay the climb; while from the cairn a panorama of mountains will be seen spread out all round the spectator. The mountaineer will be most delighted with the Northern and North-western prospect, the Cairngorms being visible from the Feshie to the Gairn. Tomintoul, on the North-eastern shoulder of Morrone has been claimed by the natives as possessing the highest arable land in the country—a distinction to which, however, it has no right.

In 1855 the Prince Consort founded a Meteorological Observatory at Castletown of Braemar. It is situated in lat. 57° 0′ N., and long. 3° 24′ W., at a height of 1114 feet above sea level. Since the death of the Prince Consort Her Majesty has maintained the Observatory in a high state of efficiency. Mr. James Aitken has been the observer for about forty years; the instruments are read twice daily, at

9 a.m. and 9 p.m. From a table of observations taken during the year 1899, we learn that August was the warmest month, with a mean temperature of 57·6° F., a highest maximum of 79·7° and a second highest minimum of 34·5°; that June and August had the lightest average winds, with a mean pressure of 0·07 lbs. per square foot; that August and June were the driest months, the former with a rain-fall of 1·3 inches in 8 days, the latter of 1·09 inches in 13 days; and that August was the month with most sunshine, totalling 213 hours 50 minutes. These facts go far to justify the visitors who crowd Braemar during August; and we may add that during the latter part of that month the hills wear in its fullest beauty their robe of imperial purple—the heather.

> Where the air that you breathe has a glorious savour,
> A birken, heathy, and piney flavour,
> All sweet commingled—not to speak
> Of a dash of the pungent, fresh peat reek.

Glen Clunie.

The road to the South from Braemar runs along the Clunie, in line with the road from Aberdeen as it enters Castletown. The distances from Clunie Bridge are: Spital of Glen Shee, 15 miles; Persie Inn, 26 miles; Bridge of Cally, 29 miles; Blairgowrie, 35 miles; Dunkeld, 47 miles. The Clunie Water rises on the North side of Cairnwell (3059 feet), on the march between the counties of Aberdeen and Perth, and has a Northerly course of about 12 miles. The road crosses the county march at an altitude of 2200 feet on the East side of Cairnwell, 10 miles from Castletown, and is a favourite route in the tourist season. Braemar is approachable on wheels only by this and the Deeside road. At Auchallater, two miles from Castletown, the Clunie receives a large tributary, the Callater Burn; close to the confluence is Coldrach:

> Coldrach Bridge,
> Where the forceful mountain torrent
> Cuts through the pointed granite ledge
> With deep, dark, swirling current.

About three miles farther South the Clunie forks, the stream on the West being called the Baddoch Burn, while that on the East is Allt Bhruididh. There are only two or three houses above Auchallater. In the upper part of the glen is Shean Spital, the most Westerly of the Deeside Spitals.

> Hail! hail! to the land where the clouds love to rest,
> Like the shroud of the dead on the mountain's cold breast;
> To the cataract's roar where the eagles reply,
> And the loch its lone bosom expands to the sky.

Glen Callater.

The Lochnagar tourist leaves the Blairgowrie road at Auchallater and enters Glen Callater, which has a somewhat desolate aspect, enlivened only by the burn as it brawls and tumbles over its rocky bed. The glen road here has been allowed to get into very bad order. The rocks are mostly of mica-slate and granite, mica-slate having been quarried at the lower end of the glen for roofing, while limestone occurs at the North-west end of Loch Callater, three miles up the glen. The loch, the water of which is tinged with peat, lies at an altitude of 1627 feet above sea level, and, covering an area of about 69 acres, has a length of nearly a mile. At the lower end is a forester's cottage, now the only house in the glen; at the upper end there is a grassy haugh, beloved of deer. Salmon are plentiful, but the sportsman has to resort to the net. A particularly large boulder at the loch side, near the cottage, indicates the position of the Priest's Well, a small chalybeate spring. According to tradition Braemar, at some remote period, suffered from a particularly severe frost, so that even on the advent of May the ground was so hard that not a plough could enter it. The priest was of course appealed to, and he led his people to this well, which even then was reputed to possess miraculous powers. Like others in the neighbourhood its waters were fast sealed up ; but, after repeated prayers the well thawed. The first water drawn was applied to holy purposes, and mass being celebrated, the thaw became general. The mountain on which the lowering clouds, intimating a change in the weather, were first seen, was accordingly named Carn an t-Sagairt, the Priest's Mountain, a designation now corrupted to Cairn Taggart; it is one of the summits of the Lochnagar group. Loch Phadruig in the neighbourhood is also said to have been named from this priest (Peter). A path leads Eastward, by the South side of Cairn Taggart, to the summit of Lochnagar, some 7 miles distant. Keeping along the loch and the burn at the upper end, Tolmount (3143 feet) will be crossed, on the other side of which lies the famous route by Jock's Road through Glen Doll. (See the author's *Lochnagar*.)

XIV.—BRAEMAR TO THE WELLS OF DEE.

Farewell, then, ye mountains in mystery piled,
  Where the birth-place and home of the tempest is found ;
Farewell ye red torrents, all foaming and wild,
  Farewell to your dreamy and desolate sound ;
Tho' o'er field, flood, and mountain my wanderings be wide,
  Back, still back, to Braemar faithful fancy shall flee,
And the beauty of Kelvin, the grandeur of Clyde,
  Shall but deepen my sigh for the banks of the Dee.

LEAVING Braemar for the West, the Deeside tourist is not without evidence that he is rapidly nearing the end of his journey. Both road and river have narrowed appreciably—the latter particularly so above its junction with the Clunie—and the glen also becomes contracted, and affords little arable land. A short series of disreputable-looking mile-stones—measuring from the Bridge of Clunie (thus ignoring the distance between that bridge and the 58th mile-stone)—also indicates the final stage of our excursion. The road skirts the base of the hill at a considerable height above the river for about four miles. As we have already seen, there are (within easy distance) to the East—Creag Choinnich, Braemar Castle, Invercauld House, the Lion's Face, and the Falls of Garbh Allt; while to the South is Morrone, and, by the Blairgowrie Road, Loch Callater and Lochnagar. To the West, keeping by the South side of the Dee, are the Falls of Corriemulzie, Inverey, the Colonel's Bed, and the Linn of Dee; while returning by the North side are Mar Lodge and the Falls of Quoich—the Dee being forded about a mile West from Castletown. This latter excursion forms a very pleasant drive from the village, which can be extended to Bynack Shieling, Geldie Lodge, or Derry Lodge. Beyond these three shooting-boxes the carriage roads become bridle paths.

The Falls of Corriemulzie, 3 miles from Castletown, are at the point where the South road crosses that little stream after its descent from Morrone. As the Falls are neared, one of the finest prospects in the Dee valley will be obtained : in the foreground, the placid river winds onward in a most deceptive manner ; its speed is much more considerable than one would at first imagine. The valley is narrow, bounded by wooded hills on both sides ; at the head also, beyond the Linn, mountains close the vista. How proudly Ravenscraig rears its crest on the South side ! It is tree-clad from base to summit, and the stately stems of the larches on the upper part of the crag are particularly noticeable. Dark pines creep up the hill faces, the foreground is relieved by birches, the green banks of the river diversified by gravelly or pebbly stretches. Often the red deer may be seen feeding by the quiet river side. In autumn the beauty of the landscape is intensified by the scarlet of the rowans, dotted here and there among the pines and birches. Indeed from Invercauld Bridge to Linn of Dee we have about eight miles of the finest glen scenery in the Highlands, and in the month of August, when the heather is in full bloom, the beauty and richness of colouring are past description. The travelled tourist who sees this section of the Valley of the Dee at its best will admit that it is one of the fairest and most magnificent scenes in the British Islands. The Falls form a beautiful slender cascade, and the sides of the miniature glen are finely clad with verdure. The heating and lighting of Mar Lodge are both effected by means of electricity. To supply the motive power the stream of Corriemulzie has been harnessed. Some distance above the Falls a large dam has been formed for the accumulation of the necessary water. At the Falls there is a headlong rush which develops fifty horse-power in the turbine, and at the adjoining power-house the dynamo develops power to the amount of 240 volts, and at the lodge, about a mile distant, 170 volts, the power being transmitted by overhead copper cables. The supply of water is utilised during the night, so that the beauty of the Falls is not interfered with.

> Ye crags and peaks . . . .
> How high you lift your heads into the sky,
> How huge you are, how mighty and how free!

Glen Quoich.

The Quoich Water joins the Dee from the North, a little to the East of the mouth of Corriemulzie Burn. The Quoich rises on the county march between Aberdeen and Banff, having Beinn a' Bhuird on the West and Ben Avon on the East, but it mostly drains the former, the chief head stream issuing from Dubh Lochan, where Pennant was informed there was ice "the latter end of July". Its Falls are about half a mile from the Dee, and by some are considered even more attractive than the Linn of Dee. A foot-bridge thrown over the stream affords a capital stand-point for viewing them. They are of no great height; it is rather in the narrow, rocky, pine-lined gorge of quartzose rock, both above and

Falls of Corriemulzie.

below the bridge, that their beauty consists. The water rushes along with great force, and makes a very fine picture, tumbling and dashing through its temporary prison. Its action has formed cavities in the rock, one of which has received the name of the Earl of Mar's Punch-bowl, and, having a resemblance to a "quaich", or cup, has given its name to the stream. Time has perforated the side of the Earl's Punch-bowl. Tradition says that this name was bestowed on it when the Earl of Mar raised his standard in Braemar, and that here he brewed a monster bowl of punch in honour of his followers. There could scarcely be a greater contrast in the course of a river than there is between the Falls and the mouth of the stream. Below the Falls the channel has been quite destroyed by the '29 and later spates, and now the Quoich spreads itself over a flattish area, which has received the name of Lochan a' Chreagain, and reluctantly enters the Dee. Glen Quoich is uninhabited, but it was by no means always so. A path leads a considerable distance up the glen, by which the ascent of Beinn a' Bhuird may be made. A cross-path connects Glen Quoich with Glen Lui by Clais na Fearna, leaving Glen Quoich about half a mile below the junction of Allt an Dubh-ghlinne with the Quoich, entering Glen Lui at the mouth of Allt a' Mhadaidh, fully a mile below Derry Lodge. Cordiner in his *North Britain* (1795) thus describes the glen: "A vast sweep of desert country, forming an immense valley, stretches up with unlimited gradations into the declivities of the surrounding mountains—decaying timber among the frequent rocks that spread the rugged soil, and lofty trees, many hoary in their fall, along the banks of the stream—express the length of years the forest has remained an uncultivated waste ".

> 'Tis a glorious glen—'tis a royal land,
> With its ridges of mountain blue;
> They rise all round, like a brother band,
> All clad in their azure hue.

Mar Lodge.

Creag an Fhithich, better known as Ravenscraig, is a beautifully wooded hill a quarter of a mile West of the Corriemulzie Falls, and had till five years ago a shooting-box on its northern slope. The original building was called Corriemulzie Cottage; on being enlarged it became known as New Mar Lodge; latterly the " New " was dropped. On its destruction by fire in 1895 the Duke of Fife decided that his Braemar seat should be on the original site on the opposite side of the Dee.

Mar Lodge, anciently called Dalmore, is opposite the 4th mile-stone, on the North side of the river, here crossed by a private bridge (the Victoria), the use of which is frequently granted to the public. The comparative lowness of its situation renders it liable to damage from floods, and the former house (now demolished) suffered considerably in the flood of '29, when the stone bridge across the Dee was carried away. The North road runs at the back of the Lodge, and a " short cut " to Glen Lui (at Black Bridge) leaves it opposite the mouth of Glen Ey. The foundation stone of the present building was laid by the Queen on 15th October, 1895, and, facing the South, it has a frontage of about 270 feet. It is sheltered on the North by a pine-clad rocky hill,

Creag a' Bhuilg, a dependency of Beinn a' Bhuird; in front, to the South, there is a broad lawn with some very fine pines. Creag Bheag, of which Creag an Fhithich is the Eastern extremity, commands the South side of the narrow valley opposite the Lodge, so that the demesne appears hill-locked on all sides. The *tout ensemble* is charming, but the architecture of the building, with its numerous gables and verandahs, is not quite in sympathy with its magnificent situation, which ranks with those of Invercauld House and Balmoral Castle. The style may be best described as Old English half-timbered, the original design having been sketched by the Duchess of Fife. The stone is coral-pink granite, and the building, which contains about 120 rooms, is roofed with small square red tiles from the English Potteries. There is a beautiful little Norman Chapel to the East; at the West is the ballroom. A deer park adjoins the Lodge on the East; it contains about 150 acres of wood, water, and pasture.

Dalmore was formerly the property of a family of Mackenzies, having been granted, according to tradition, by James IV. to two natural sons of Kenneth, 9th Earl of Kintail. After the Rebellion of 1715 the Mackenzies had to part with their lands to the first Earl of Fife. The "Gallows Tree" is situated a short distance West of Victoria Bridge, and may easily be seen from the South road right above a large gravel pit.

What lonely magnificence stretches around!
Each sight how sublime! and how awful each sound!
All hushed and serene, as a region of dreams,
The mountains repose 'mid the roar of the streams.

Inverey. Inverey lies on both sides of the Ey Burn near its confluence with the Dee. The hamlet on the East side is distinguished as Meikle Inverey, that on the West as Little Inverey—the latter being 5 miles from Braemar. Till very recently Inverey was a fine example of a distinctly Highland clachan, but it is advancing with the times, and houses of a better class are springing up. The ruins of an old castle of the Farquharsons of Inverey are still standing in Meikle Inverey, with the "Gallows Tree" in front. The castle was burned by the royal forces after the battle of Killiecrankie. The Inverey Farquharsons would appear to have outlived their time, clinging with almost fatal persistence to the "divine right" of Highland "gentlemen" to descend on the richer Lowlanders and "lift" their cattle. The Invercauld Farquharsons would seem to have adapted themselves more promptly to altered times, even taking the liberty of hanging, for a slight misdemeanour, one of their Inverey cousins. The latter objected to the proceeding on its merits, as well as to the indignity of being suspended on his own "Tree", but without avail. He is said to have prophesied that his "Tree" would be standing when the Farquharsons of Invercauld should have disappeared; the Tree remains, but the direct male line of Invercauld, as already noted, has died out. Near the mouth of the burn is a disused and neglected old burying ground, the remotest on Deeside, where rest forgotten generations of the hardy old Celts, with

> The green Quadrangle of the hills
> to watch their sleep profound,
> And the Gaudeamus of the burns
> making a homely sound.

Glen Ey is about 7 miles long, the Ey rising on the Ben Uarns (Beinn Iutharn Mhor, 3424 feet, and Beinn Iutharn Bheag, 3011 feet), the "mountains of hell". About a mile and a half up the glen is a much-visited spot, the Colonel's Bed, a narrow, rocky gorge, through which the Ey flows. Here John Farquharson of Inverey, the Black Colonel, lay in concealment for some time after the battle of Killiecrankie. His "Bed"—a mere recess on a rocky shelf—must have been rather hard and unpleasant, although tradition says he was not always without agreeable company. His Annie Bhan, however, passed away, and was laid to rest in Inverey churchyard, where, shortly before his death, he gave orders for his own interment. His relations, naturally enough, did not see the propriety of this arrangement, preferring the family burial ground at Castletown. But the corpse was obstinate, and again and again was to be found of a morning above ground. At last his widow yielded to supernatural powers, and the body was transferred to Inverey. The coffin, says the tradition, was towed up the river with a horse-hair rope. The natives have added to the "furniture" of the Colonel's quarters, and point out to visitors his table—a rock in the stream below the Bed—and wash-hand basin—a water-worn hollow in a boulder above the Bed—both having a certain rude appropriateness for their suggested use. The Colonel's "Cave" is on Creag a' Chait, a little above the junction of the Allt Connie with the Ey. The Allt Connie is a lively little burn, with pretty falls and rapids. About half a mile above the Colonel's Bed is Aucherrie, the only inhabited house in the glen above Inverey. Near the head of the glen is Alltanodhar Shieling, a small shooting-box in connection with the Glen Ey portion of the Forest of Mar, seldom occupied in recent years. The road does not go beyond this Shieling, but a way is sometimes made to the head of the glen and thence to Spital of Glen Shee.

> Under Linn of Dee, over rocks, between rocks,
> Freed from prison the river comes, pouring, rolling, rushing,
> Then at a sudden descent goes sliding, gliding, unbroken,
> Falling, sliding, gliding, in narrow space confined,
> Save for a curl at the end where the curve rejoins the level,
> Save for a ripple at last, a sheeted descent unbroken.

Linn of Dee.

The Linn of Dee, a few yards past the 6th mile-stone, the terminus of many an excursion, next claims attention. Those who visit the Linn for the first time expecting to see a great "fall" will be disappointed, though picturesqueness and grandeur are by no means wanting. The Linn is a unique spot, not yielding all its beauties to a casual glance. Here, 1243 feet above sea level, in as narrow a prison as ever temporarily "cribbed, cabined, and confined" a river, the Dee hastens forward, seething, churning, and rushing with, as it were, the impetuosity of youth and the strength of maturity. The never-ending turbulent rush of the river along a rock-bound channel of about 80 yards in length and in some places less than four feet in breadth, makes a great impression on the beholder. In the thousands of years during which this battle of waters has been fought, the Dee has smoothed and polished the sides of the gorge, yet has not reduced them to uniformity, for the curves of many a "pot-hole" may be seen in the sides of the gorge. Having

Linn of Dee.

successfully struggled for the right of passage, determined not to be turned aside, the fury of the river subsides as quickly at the lower end as it was aroused at the upper end of the prison-channel. A pool, 40 feet deep, receives the troubled stream, leaving which it broadens and ripples demurely along. A shoal of salmon may frequently be seen in the pool, dull and listless, and often closely packed together, recuperating themselves for a final tussle with the opposing rush. And in due time the successful leap is at last made. In the beginning of the present century a plank did duty as a means of communication across the Dee here, being replaced, about 1830, by "an alpine wooden bridge, at a height of 30 feet above the stream". The latter was succeeded by the present handsome granite structure, opened by the Queen in 1857; though sometimes one thinks that the "auld, ricketty, widden brig" better became the scene than the fine modern arch. Here the South Deeside road ends. Her Majesty occasionally extends her drives as far as the Linn.

From Moore's *Life of Byron* we learn that the poet nearly lost his life while on a visit to the Linn. "As he was", says Moore, "scrambling along a declivity that overhangs the fall, some heather caught his lame foot and he fell. Already he was rolling downwards, when the attendant luckily caught hold of him, and was but just in time to save him from being killed".

Looking Westward from the bridge, the prospect appears to have suddenly changed, and we receive an impression that the end of our journey is approaching. Not that the river is insignificantly small, but cultivation suddenly ceases, and the forester reigns solitary and supreme. Deer are numerous, for the Forest of Mar is the largest in Scotland, and second to none for sheltering corries and woods. As it is comparatively little shot over, the denizens of the adjoining forests frequently seek sanctuary by the head-streams of the Dee.

> The scenes are desert now and bare
> Where flourished once a forest fair.

Glen Lui.

The Lui Water, an important tributary, joins the Dee fully half a mile below the Linn. The Lui is formed by the junction of two burns from the Cairngorms—the Luibeg from the Lochan Uaine of Ben Muich Dhui and the Southern slopes of that mountain, and the Derry from Loch Etchachan and the Eastern face of the monarch of the Cairngorms. The Lui is crossed near its mouth by a bridge in connection with the North Deeside road, a little above which are two pretty waterfalls, rarely visited because not easily accessible. There are only two houses in Glen Lui—Derry Lodge and Luibeg Cottage near the confluence of the Derry and the Luibeg Burns—both used in working Mar Forest. An excellent forest road, always open to the public, connects Derry Lodge with the North road, crossing the Lui at Black Bridge about a mile and a half from the Linn. At Black Bridge, where a direct road branches off to Mar Lodge, there are some fine old pines, sturdy monarchs of the glen. But hurricanes have devastated the glen in the lower portion; in the upper young plantations are promising. There is now no arable land in the glen, but many *larachs* will be observed on both sides of the stream, especially on the left. At Derry Lodge, about 10 miles from Braemar, two tracks lead farther into the mountains. The path on the right (North), up Glen Derry, is part of an old drove road, the Learg an Laoigh (the calves' pass), separating the Central Cairngorms from the Eastern, leading over the river Avon and, rounding Ben Bynac, along the Nethy to Speyside. (Nethy Bridge, 32 miles from Braemar.) The path on the left (West) leads up the lower part of Glen Luibeg, and then crosses into Glen Dee opposite the Devil's Point, rounding Carn a' Mhaim, the Southerly spur of Ben Muich Dhui. (Aviemore, 30 miles from Braemar.) This route is generally preferred by tourists to that by White Bridge. At the mouth of Glen Derry, over a century ago, the Earl of Fife generously left a shieling open for the convenience of passing drovers and others—an arrangement, however, which we read had to be ended owing to the "depredations of poachers". In the lower part of the glen there are still a few noble pines, worthy successors of the hundred-feet monarchs that a hundred years ago made the head-streams of the Dee famous for firs; but two miles beyond the Lodge storm-bleached trunks only are to be found. A well-known Deeside character, Alexander Davidson (1792-1843), purchased much of the timber in the Derry, and constructed a Dam in the upper end of the glen for floating cut trees to the Dee. "Rough Sanie", as he was called from his long, black, unkempt beard, however, was unfortunate; what he had earned in smuggling disappeared in the timber speculation. Ultimately he became notorious as a poacher. The flood of

1829 made an end of the Dam, but traces of it are still visible. Among the mountains that slope to Glen Derry may be named Derry Cairngorm (3788 feet) and Beinn Mheadhoin (3883 feet), the former remarkable for its conical summit, the latter for its "warty" ridge. Derry Cairngorm also possesses a Lochan Uaine with a burn, Allt an Lochan Uaine, immortalised in a poem of that name by William Smith, an Abernethy poet and "deer-stalker", who had a turf hut there for his own use when "chasing the red deer" on the Cairngorms. Some of Smith's songs are said to breathe the very essence of poetry; he ultimately served under Sir John Moore. The Queen went up Glen Derry twice—on 7th October, 1859, to Ben Muich Dhui, and on 28th September, 1861, to Loch Avon. Carn Crom fills up the angle between Glen Derry and Glen Luibeg and is noted for a corrie, Coire na Craoibh Ora (the gold tree corrie), so named from a Mackenzie of Dalmore having, according to tradition, buried a bag of gold here.

> There's nothing left to fancy's guess,
> You see that all is loneliness:
> And silence aids—though the steep hills
> Send to the glen a thousand rills.

Glen Dee.

The valley of the Dee below the Linn is frequently called Strathdee, the name "Glen Dee" being restricted to the portion above. The North road is continued along the river till it crosses the Dee, 9 miles from Castletown, at White Bridge, a wooden structure a few yards above the mouth of the Geldie Burn, the Dee's largest tributary from the West.

Indeed, some have held that the Geldie (White Dee) is the real head-stream of the river, seeing that it flows in the general Eastward course of the Dee. It is, however, considerably inferior both in volume and length to the stream which White Bridge crosses. It is doubtful, notwithstanding the occasional white stony channel, if the name "Geldie" is appropriate, for the first peaty water that enters the Dee is brought by it. Rising between An Sgarsoch (3300 feet) and Carn an Fhidleir (3276 feet)—the latter mountain at the junction of three counties, Aberdeen, Perth, and Inverness—it flows rather languidly for several miles along a flat and mossy glen. An Sgarsoch is a flat-topped hill, with grassy slopes, where formerly a cattle market was held. This "Tryst" was the successor to a market previously held in Glen Feshie; latterly it was removed still farther South, till it ultimately became stationary at Falkirk. Geldie Lodge, the most Westerly house in Aberdeenshire, is on the right bank of the burn, at the mouth of Allt Coire an t-Seilich, about four miles from White Bridge. It is a shooting-box in connection with the Geldie portion of the Mar Forest. Glen Geldie is rather flat and uninteresting, the nearer hills on each side being generally low and bare; the Queen describes it as "a moor which was so soft and boggy in places that we had to get off several times. The hills were wild but not very high, bare of trees and even of heather to a great extent". One of the Geldie's tributaries, the Bynack Burn, rises on the Perthshire boundary, near the head of Glen Tilt. On the right bank of that burn, about two miles from White Bridge, there is another small shooting-box, Bynack Shieling. The two principal left-bank tributaries of the Geldie are Allt Dhaidh Mor and Allt Dhaidh Beag, the former rising on Beinn Bhrotain, the latter on Carn-Cloich-mhuilinn (3087 feet). Between these burns is Duke's Chair (2010 feet), a hill which received name from the Duke of Leeds when tenant of Mar Forest; East of Duke's Chair is Carn Geldie (2039 feet) with Cnapan Ora. The latter name recalls the incident in Coire na Craoibh Ora, from which corrie the laird removed his gold to Carn Geldie, depositing it under a boulder on which he cut the figure of a horse-shoe—and there it still remains! Bridle paths lead from Geldie Lodge to Glen Feshie, and from Bynack Shieling to Glen Tilt. Kingussie is 32 miles distant from Braemar *via* Glen Feshie; and Blair Athole *via* Glen Tilt 30 miles.

About midway between Linn of Dee and the Geldie, on the South side of the river, are Dail a' Mhoraire Bheag and Dail a' Mhoraire Mhor (Dalavorar)—the little and big lord's haugh. The buildings are now in ruins. On the same side of the river, but farther West, is Dubh-bhruach (Dubrach), where a sergeant's guard was stationed after the Rebellion of 1745. A forester's house or two near the junction of the Bynack Burn with the Geldie make the desolation of this region only the more apparent.

> A scene so wild, so rude as this,
> Yet so sublime in barrenness,
> Ne'er did my wandering footsteps press.

Learg Ghruamach.

The rough mountain track up Glen Dee from White Bridge, passing the Pools of Dee, and ending at Coylum Bridge, near Aviemore, is an ancient right-of-way betwixt Deeside and Speyside. Dividing the Central from the Western Cairngorms, it is known to mountaineers as the Larig Ghru, a contraction of Learg Ghruamach (the gruesome pass), a name which fitly describes its character—hemmed in as it is by mountains rising 2000 feet above it. About half a mile Westward from the confluence of the Geldie with the Dee, there is a noted rapid known as the Chest of Dee. This is a narrow, rock-bound part of the river,

Chest of Dee.

about 120 yards long, graced with a few birches, having three distinct step-like falls into a pool. Leaving this pool, the river takes one more "step" and is free. The falls are very slight indeed, but the motion imparted to the imprisoned water so agitates the river here that it frets and "splutters" in a very lively manner. There was a foot-bridge over the Dee here before White Bridge was built; the ford was nearer the junction of the Geldie with the Dee—the stones are still visible. At Coire na Cula, a mile and a half above White Bridge, may be seen the *larach* of a building said to mark the site of the uppermost hunting seat of the Earls of Mar. The great mass of Beinn Bhrotain, the culminating height on the right bank of the Dee between the Geldie and the Geusachan, will be noticed on the left; on the right is Sgor Mor (2666 feet) the highest summit of the outskirts of the Cairngorms that lie between the Dee and the Lui. Now within sight of

> the grisly cliffs which guard
> The infant rills of Highland Dee,

we observe on our right the path from Derry Lodge entering the Larig opposite the Devil's Point. Dr. Skene Keith tells us that in his time (1810) "the only human habitation [in this neighbourhood] was a shealing, belonging to some farmers in Badenoch, who rent these glens from Earl Fife, and where shepherds reside a few months in summer". The shieling has been displaced by a "watcher's" hut, Corrour, at the foot of the Devil's Point, and the sheep-farmers by deer-stalkers. Proceeding by the stony track we cross Allt Clach nan Taillear, passing, about three-quarters of a mile South of its confluence, several boulders, piled together, known as Clach nan Taillear (the tailor's stone), so named from three Rothiemurchus tailors who perished here on their way to Dalmore. According to tradition they wagered they would dance at three "Dales" within twenty-four hours, and having performed two-thirds of their programme at Abernethy and Rothiemurchus sank exhausted in the snow at this spot.

Proceeding towards the water-shed we pass the confluence of the Garchary and the Larig Burn—where at one time, notwithstanding the altitude (about 2000 feet), pines flourished—and so reach the Pools of Dee, near the lowermost of which a bridle path will be descried on the left leading towards the summit of Braeriach and the Wells of Dee, where

> From the bosom of the mountain,
> From the silent lands of night,
> Sparkles up the infant fountain,
> Crystal clear and crowned with light.

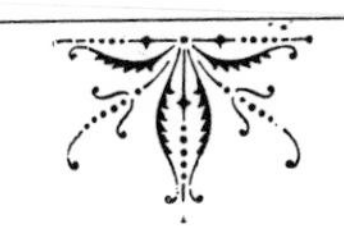

INDEX.

Dark figures (thus **23**) denote the page referring more particularly to the subject.

By Special Appointment
to
THE QUEEN
and
H·R·H· THE PRINCE OF WALES

DAVID McHARDY & SON

FURNISHING IRONMONGERS,

BELL HANGERS AND MANUFACTURERS
OF
GENERAL SMITH WORK,

54 Netherkirkgate, ABERDEEN.

ESTABLISHED 1797